AF889103

Published by Fusion Dynamics and You LLC
www.fdyconsultants.com

ISBN: 97-1-960973-02-3

Disclaimer: The information provided in this book is for educational purposes only and should not be construed as financial advice. Before making any financial decisions or committing to any strategies or opportunities discussed, we strongly recommend consulting with a qualified financial planner or advisor. They can assess your individual circumstances and help guide you in making informed decisions that align with your financial goals and needs.

Dr. Kindall M. Bundy, MBA, QMHP, CDP, CWC
FD&Y Consultants

Table of CONTENTS

Table of

CONTENTS

FD&Y Consultants

YOUR VISION IS OUR MISSION

Dr. Kindall Bundy has been at the forefront of business innovation for over 20 years, contributing significantly to the growth and development of organizations across the Richmond, Virginia area. With a deep passion for progress, Dr. Bundy consistently seeks to expand the boundaries of business practices through dedicated research, exploration, and the implementation of strategic resources. This drive culminated in the establishment of FD&Y Consultants, a firm committed to offering essential guidance to young professionals, individuals, and organizations. Dr. Bundy's expertise focuses on fostering skill development, advancing forward-thinking business strategies, promoting independent growth, enhancing community engagement, providing critical resources, and supporting effective succession planning.

DR. KINDALL M. BUNDY, MBA, QMHP, CDP,CWC
CEO & Founder of FD&Y Consultants

INTRODUCTION

WHY PERSONAL FINANCE MATTERS

Personal finance management is crucial for achieving financial stability and long-term success. By effectively budgeting, saving, and investing, individuals can work towards their purchase goals and ensure they have the resources to cover both planned and unexpected expenses. Managing debt is equally important, as it allows for financial freedom and avoids unnecessary stress. A positive mindset toward these practices can empower individuals to make informed decisions, avoid financial pitfalls, and stay focused on their long-term goals, ultimately leading to a secure and fulfilling financial future.

WHAT THIS TOOLKIT WILL TEACH YOU

In this toolkit, we'll break down personal finance into simple, actionable steps. You'll learn how to:

- Create a budget that works for you, not against you.
- Start investing, even if you're a complete beginner.
- Build savings that safeguard your future.
- Plan for big goals, like buying a home, starting a family, or retiring comfortably.
- Manage debt strategically without feeling overwhelmed.
- Develop a positive mindset around money to reduce stress and build confidence.

Whether you're just starting your financial journey or looking for ways to refine your strategies, there's something here for everyone.

WHY PERSONAL FINANCE MATTERS

PERSONAL FINANCE MANAGEMENT

Personal finance management is important for several reasons, as it directly impacts both short-term and long-term financial well-being. Here are some key reasons why managing personal finances matters:

1. Financial Security

Proper money management helps ensure you have enough to cover your basic needs, such as housing, food, and utilities. It also creates a safety net for emergencies, like unexpected medical expenses or job loss. This can reduce stress and anxiety about financial instability.

2. Debt Prevention

Effective personal finance management helps prevent accumulating excessive debt. By budgeting, saving, and planning for purchases, you can avoid relying on credit cards or loans, which can lead to high-interest payments and financial stress.

3. Achieving Financial Goals

Whether you're saving for a home, a car, education, or retirement, good financial management helps you set clear goals and create a plan to achieve them. It allows you to allocate money wisely toward these goals and track your progress.

4. Building Savings and Investments

When you manage your finances well, you're more likely to have the discipline to save and invest. This leads to building wealth over time through savings accounts, stocks, bonds, or retirement funds. Investments can generate passive income and provide for future financial needs.

5. Retirement Planning

Managing your finances allows you to start saving for retirement early, taking advantage of compound interest and growing your wealth over time. It ensures that you're financially prepared for the future and can maintain your standard of living in retirement.

6. Reducing Financial Stress

One of the biggest causes of stress is financial uncertainty. By budgeting, tracking spending, and saving, you take control of your money and reduce the anxiety that comes with worrying about paying bills or making ends meet.

7. Increased Financial Freedom

Managing your money allows you to make choices based on your priorities and desires, rather than being constrained by financial limitations. When you're financially responsible, you're more likely to have the flexibility to travel, pursue hobbies, or make major life changes.

8. Improved Credit Score

Personal finance management helps maintain a good credit score by paying bills on time, keeping debt levels manageable, and avoiding late fees. A good credit score can open doors for better loan rates, mortgages, and other financial opportunities.

9. Empowerment and Confidence

When you manage your finances well, it gives you a sense of control and empowerment. Knowing you're in charge of your financial situation can boost your confidence in making financial decisions and in navigating unexpected situations.

10. Preventing Lifestyle Inflation

As your income increases, it's easy to spend more, leading to lifestyle inflation. Proper financial management helps you avoid this so that increased income goes toward long-term goals, savings, and investments instead of higher daily expenses.

In short, personal finance management is essential for both peace of mind and building a stable, successful financial future. It helps you achieve your goals, manage risks, and ensure you are prepared for both planned and unexpected life events.

WHY WAIT TO START...?

The sooner you start saving, the more financial security and peace of mind you'll have in the future. Waiting to save money often leads to missed opportunities, as the power of compound interest grows stronger over time. By making small, consistent contributions to your savings today, you're laying the foundation for a stable financial future, whether it's for emergencies, retirement, or achieving your goals. Starting now not only builds your financial resilience but also ensures that you're prepared for unexpected expenses. Don't wait for the "perfect time" — the best time to begin securing your financial future is right now.

HOW TO USE THIS TOOLKIT

Each chapter focuses on a core aspect of personal finance. At the end of each chapter, you'll find:

KEY TAKEAWAYS

A summary of the main points.

ACTION STEPS

Simple tasks you can do right away to apply what you've learned.

RESOURCES

Recommendations for tools, apps, or further reading.

Keep this toolkit as a helpful resource to refer back to whenever you need guidance. Begin with the chapter that resonates most with your current needs, or read through the entire guide to develop a comprehensive plan.

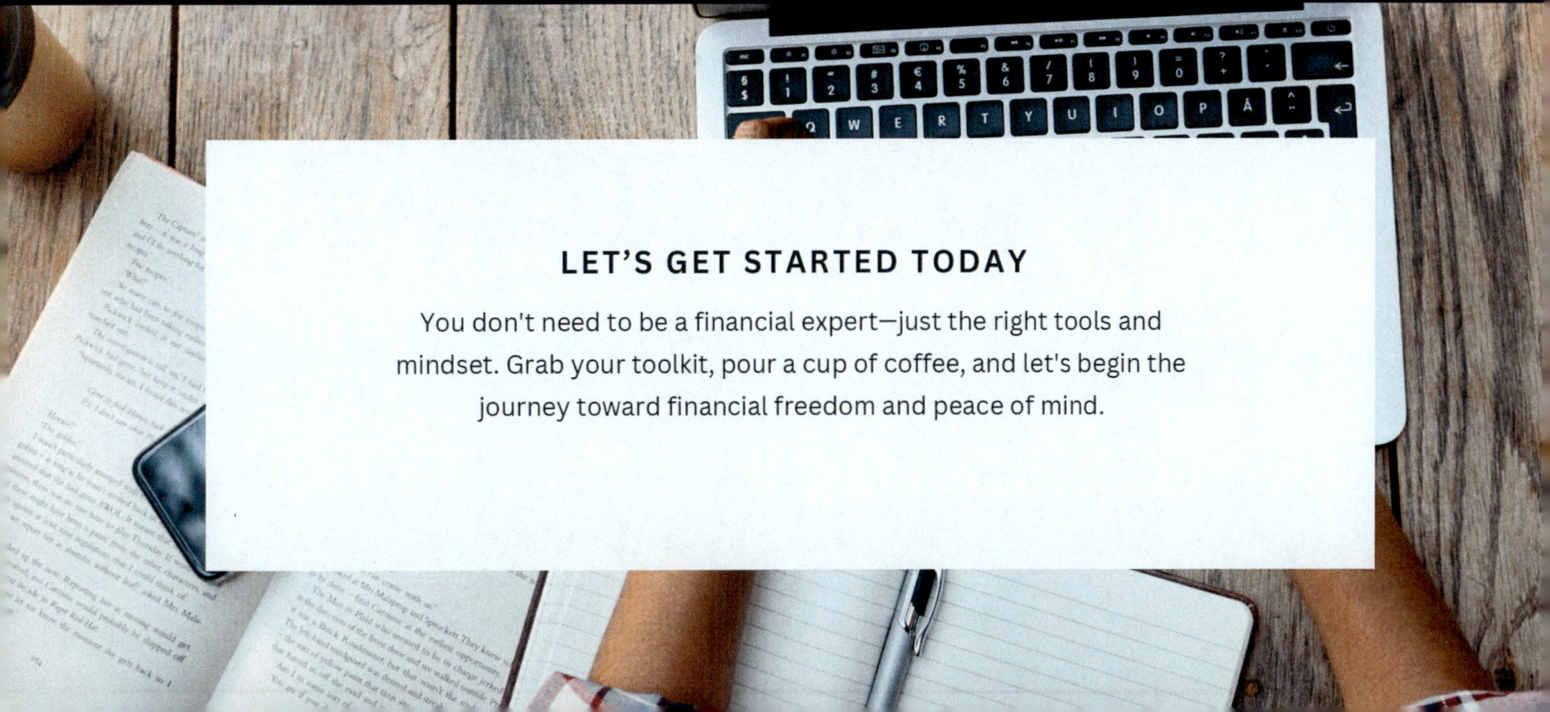

LET'S GET STARTED TODAY

You don't need to be a financial expert—just the right tools and mindset. Grab your toolkit, pour a cup of coffee, and let's begin the journey toward financial freedom and peace of mind.

CHAPTER 01

UNDERSTANDING YOUR CURRENT FINANCIAL STATUS

CHAPTER 01

UNDERSTANDING YOUR FINANCIAL SITUATION

"You Can't Fix What You Don't Measure"

Before you can take control of your finances, it's crucial to understand where you currently stand. Think of this step as a financial check-up it is about gathering a clear picture of your income, expenses, assets, and liabilities. With this foundation, you can identify what's working, what needs improvement, and where to focus your efforts.

STEP 01

Assess Your Income

Your income is the starting point for building your financial plan. This includes:

- **Primary Income:** Your salary, wages, or consistent earnings from a main job.
- **Additional Income:** Freelance work, side hustles, rental income, or any other sources.

ACTION STEP:

List all your sources of income and their amounts. Use a monthly total for consistency.

- **Gather Documentation:** Collect all relevant income statements, such as pay stubs, tax returns, bank statements, or records of any additional sources of income (e.g., freelance work, side gigs, investments).
- **Identify All Sources of Income:** List every source of income you receive, including your salary, business income, rental income, interest, dividends, or any other streams of money.
- **Calculate Gross Income:** Determine your total income before taxes or deductions. This includes regular wages, bonuses, commissions, and any additional earnings.
- **Identify Opportunities for Increasing Income:** Look for ways to increase your income, such as seeking a raise, finding a higher-paying job, pursuing additional side income, or investing in skill development.

STEP 02

Track Your Expenses

Tracking your expenses is a powerful way to understand where your money is going each month. Breaking your expenses into categories can give you a clearer picture and help you identify areas for improvement. Here are some common categories to consider:

- **Fixed Expenses:** Rent, mortgage, insurance, and other recurring costs.
- **Variable Expenses:** Groceries, entertainment, utilities, and transportation.
- **Discretionary Spending:** Dining out, subscriptions, shopping, and hobbies.

ACTION STEP:

- **Track Income Over Time:** Keep a record of your income over several months or years to spot trends, assess your financial progress, and make informed decisions for future financial planning.
- **Assess Your Income Against Expenses:** Compare your income to your monthly expenses to identify any gaps or areas for improvement. This can help you determine if you're living within your means or if adjustments are necessary.
- **Review:** Look at the past three months of bank statements and categorize your spending. Use apps like Mint or You Need a Budget (YNAB) for automated tracking.
- **Track Income Over Time:** Keep a record of your income over several months or years to spot trends, assess your financial progress, and make informed decisions for future financial planning.

STEP 03

Calculate Your Net Worth

Your net worth is a snapshot of your financial health. It's calculated by subtracting what you owe (liabilities) from what you own (assets).

ASSETS INCLUDE:

- **Cash and savings:** Money in bank accounts, savings accounts, or emergency funds.
- **Investments**: Stocks, bonds, retirement accounts (401(k), IRA), and other investments.
- **Property:** The value of your home, real estate, or other valuable property.
- **Personal property:** Cars, jewelry, art, collectibles, or other valuable personal items.
- **Business ownership:** If you own a business, the value of your business.

LIABILITIES INCLUDE:

- **Mortgages:** Remaining balance on your home loan.
- **Credit card debt:** Total balances on credit cards.
- **Student loans:** Remaining balance on student loans.
- **Car loans:** Remaining balance on auto loans.
- **Personal loans:** Any other loans or outstanding debts.

FORMULA: Net Worth = Total Assets - Total Liabilities

ACTION STEP:

- Create a simple table listing your assets and liabilities to calculate your net worth. This is your starting point—it's not about judgment, just awareness.
- Tracking your net worth over time helps you measure your financial progress and identify areas for improvement.

STEP 04

Analyze Your Spending Patterns

Once you've tracked your expenses, identify patterns. Are there areas where you're overspending? Are you allocating enough toward savings and investments?

COMMON INSIGHTS:

Look at each category and ask yourself the following questions:

- **Necessity:** Is this purchase essential? Are there areas where you're overspending on non-essential items?
- **Frequency:** Are these purchases recurring (e.g., monthly subscriptions) or occasional? How often are you spending on these items?
- **Comparison**: Compare your spending against budget guidelines or averages for your income level. Are there categories where you're spending too much?

ACTION STEP:

Identify Trends and Patterns

Examine your spending over time to spot trends. For example:

- **Consistency:** Do you find that certain categories (e.g., food, entertainment, or shopping) remain consistently high month after month?
- **Irregularities:** Are there impulse purchases or unexpected large expenses that disrupt your budget?
- **Seasonal patterns:** Do your expenses increase around holidays, birthdays, or vacations? How can you plan for these fluctuations in the future?

STEP 05

Set a Baseline for Improvement

Now that you know your income, expenses, net worth, and spending patterns, set a baseline for improvement.

KEY METRICS TO MONITOR:

- **Savings rate:** How much are you saving each month as a percentage of your income?
- **Debt-to-income ratio:** The percentage of your income that goes toward paying debt.
- **Net worth:** Track this over time to measure progress.

ACTION STEP:

- Commit to tracking these metrics monthly or quarterly to stay accountable.
- Review your spending regularly (monthly or quarterly) to ensure you're staying within your budget and making progress toward your financial goals. Reassess your spending patterns if needed and adjust accordingly.

KEY TAKEAWAYS

- Understanding your current financial situation is the first step toward improvement.
- Income, expenses, and net worth are the three pillars of your financial foundation.
- Small, consistent changes in spending or saving can lead to significant progress over time.

ACTION STEPS TO TAKE NOW:

- Gather your income details and calculate your monthly total.
- Track your expenses for the past three months and categorize them.
- Create a net worth statement by listing all assets and liabilities.
- Identify 1–2 areas to improve and write down specific actions to take this month.

Asset vs. Liability

Break Down:

ASSET VS LIABILITY

Why Are Assets Important?
Assets are crucial because they help you build wealth, secure your financial future, and provide income or capital for growth. Having a portfolio of assets increases your financial stability and independence. Assets can generate passive income, increase value (appreciation), and protect you against inflation or unexpected expenses.

Assets are things that provide value and help you create wealth. These can include cash, property, investments, equipment, or anything that can generate income or appreciate over time. In personal finance, assets are items that put money in your pocket.

Liabilities, on the other hand, are financial obligations that take money out of your pocket. These can include loans, credit card debts, mortgages, or any other debt you owe. Essentially, liabilities are things that represent a future financial burden.

Finding Balance Between Assets and Liabilities:
The balance between assets and liabilities is key to financial health. You want to ensure that your assets outweigh your liabilities so that your net worth remains positive. Here's how you can find balance:

1. **Maximize Asset Accumulation:** Focus on increasing assets that can be appreciated (like real estate, stocks, or business investments).
2. **Minimize Liability:** Try to pay down high-interest debts (like credit card debt) and avoid acquiring liabilities that don't produce income.
3. **Leverage Good Debt:** Not all debt is bad. For example, a mortgage for a property that appreciates can be considered "good debt" if the value of the property increases over time.

The goal is to have your assets generate enough income or value to cover your liabilities and create wealth.

Worst Liabilities to Have:

The worst liabilities are those that drain your finances without providing any benefit or growth. Some of the worst include:

- **High-Interest Debt:** Credit cards and payday loans with high-interest rates can quickly spiral out of control, leading to substantial financial strain.
- **Unnecessary Consumer Debt:** Loans taken to fund lifestyle choices that don't generate income (like buying a car you can't afford) are liabilities that depreciate in value quickly.
- **Personal Loans for Non-Essentials:** Borrowing for things like vacations or non-investment purchases that don't improve your future financial situation.
- **Debt that Cannot Be Paid Off Easily:** Certain loans, such as student loans with high interest, may be difficult to manage if not handled properly, especially if the income from the related investment (like education) doesn't provide the expected return.

Controlling the Appreciation of Your Assets

To control the appreciation of your assets, consider the following strategies:

- **Invest in High-Return Assets:** Focus on assets that tend to appreciate, such as real estate, stocks, bonds, or even businesses. Diversifying your investments can help protect against risks and ensure steady growth.
- **Regular Maintenance and Upkeep:** For physical assets like property, regular maintenance can ensure that their value doesn't deteriorate. Keeping your assets in good condition prevents depreciation and ensures they continue to appreciate.
- **Invest in Education and Skill Development:** Personal development can be an asset that appreciates over time. Skills and knowledge increase your earning potential, which translates into increased net worth.
- **Monitor the Market and Act Early:** For assets like stocks, real estate, or collectibles, monitoring the market trends and making informed decisions about when to buy, sell, or hold can maximize their appreciation.

In short, focus on acquiring assets that generate positive cash flow, minimize liabilities, and keep a close eye on maintaining and nurturing your assets to ensure their long-term growth and appreciation.

PERSONAL FINANCE

LEARN TO MASTER YOUR MONEY & IMPROVE YOUR LIFE

CHAPTER 02

BUDGETING

CHAPTER 02

BUDGETING

"People don't plan to fail, they fail to plan"

The phrase "People don't plan to fail, they fail to plan" highlights the importance of intentional preparation in achieving success. It suggests that most people don't deliberately set themselves up for failure; rather, they neglect to make a clear plan or strategy, which leads to unintended consequences. Without a solid plan, it's easy to get off track, waste time, or miss opportunities. Planning helps you stay focused, set goals, and make informed decisions, ultimately leading to better outcomes in both your personal and professional life.

Why Budgeting Matters

A well-crafted budget is not about limiting yourself; it's about giving you control over your finances. By understanding how much you earn, spend, and save, you can reduce stress, manage debt, and reach your goals more efficiently. Whether you're saving for a major purchase, building an emergency fund, or planning for retirement, a budget acts as a roadmap to help you stay on track and make informed financial decisions.

How to Create a Budget

Start by calculating your monthly income after taxes, as this is the foundation for your budget. Next, categorize your expenses into fixed costs (like rent, insurance, and subscriptions) and variable costs (such as groceries, utilities, and transportation), which can fluctuate. Allocate funds for discretionary spending, like dining out or entertainment. After defining your categories, assign specific amounts to each, ensuring that your total expenses don't exceed your income. If they do, adjust your spending by cutting back on non-essential items to stay within budget.

Popular Budgeting Methods

Budgeting isn't one-size-fits-all. Here are a few approaches to consider:

50/30/20 RULE

Allocate 50% of your income to needs, 30% to wants, and 20% to savings or debt repayment. This simple method works well for beginners.

ZERO-BASED BUDGETING

Every dollar you earn has a job, whether it's paying a bill, funding savings, or investing. At the end of the month, your income minus expenses should equal zero.

ENVELOPE SYSTEM

Set aside cash for specific categories, like groceries or entertainment, in physical envelopes. Once the envelope is empty, you stop spending in that category for the month.

Experiment with these methods to find one that aligns with your goals and lifestyle.

Making Your Budget Work

A successful budget is built on flexibility, as unexpected expenses are a part of life. It's important to review your budget regularly, whether weekly or monthly, and make adjustments when necessary. Celebrate small wins, such as staying within your grocery budget or saving extra money, as these successes boost your confidence and momentum. If consistency is a challenge, budgeting apps like Mint, YNAB, or PocketGuard can help by automating much of the process and providing real-time insights into your spending habits.

50/30/20 Rule

Break Down:

50/30/20 RULE

Allocate 50% of your income to needs, 30% to wants, and 20% to savings or debt repayment. This simple method works well for beginners.

The 50/30/20 rule is a popular and straightforward budgeting method, especially for those just starting out with managing their finances. Here's a breakdown of how it works:

- 50% to Needs: This portion covers your essential expenses, like rent or mortgage, utilities, groceries, insurance, transportation, and minimum debt payments. These are the non-negotiable costs that you need to live.

- 30% to Wants: This category includes everything that's not essential but enhances your lifestyle. Think dining out, entertainment, shopping for clothes, hobbies, vacations, or any other non-essential spending.

- 20% to Savings or Debt Repayment: This portion should be focused on building an emergency fund, contributing to retirement savings, or paying off debts. If you're in debt, prioritize repaying high-interest debt first to avoid paying more in the long run.

For example, if your monthly income is $3,000:

- 50% for Needs: $1,500
- 30% for Wants: $900
- 20% for Savings/Debt Repayment: $600

This method helps to balance your spending between necessary expenses, personal enjoyment, and financial security, and it’s flexible enough to adjust as your financial situation changes. Would you like tips on how to start budgeting or tracking these categories effectively?

Zero-Based Budgeting

Break Down:

ZERO-BASED BUDGETING

Every dollar you earn has a job, whether it's paying a bill, funding savings, or investing. At the end of the month, your income minus expenses should equal zero.

This concept is often called "zero-based budgeting." The idea is that every dollar you earn should be assigned a specific purpose by the end of the month, so your income minus your expenses equals zero. The goal isn't necessarily to have "nothing left," but rather to ensure that every dollar has a "job" — whether it's going toward bills, savings, investments, or even fun expenses.

Here's how it works in practice:

1. List All Income

Start by calculating your total monthly income. This includes your salary, side gigs, or any other sources of income.

2. Categorize Your Expenses

List all of your expenses, both fixed (like rent or mortgage, utilities, and car payments) and variable (like groceries, entertainment, or clothing). Don't forget savings or debt repayment, which are also considered expenses in this budgeting method.

3. Assign Each Dollar a Job

Take the total income and allocate it across all categories, ensuring that every dollar has a place. This means that once you've assigned all your income to bills, savings, or wants, your balance should be $0.

For example, if you earn $3,000 a month:

- Rent: $1,000
- Utilities: $200
- Groceries: $300
- Entertainment: $150
- Savings: $500
- Debt Repayment: $300
- Miscellaneous: $550

At the end of the month, your income minus your expenses should equal zero, with all funds having been assigned a purpose. If there's extra money in one category, it could be reallocated to another, such as increasing savings or paying off more debt.

Benefits:

- Better control: You're intentionally planning how every dollar is spent, which reduces the chance of overspending.
- Increased savings: By assigning a portion of your income to savings or debt repayment, it ensures you're prioritizing your financial goals.
- Financial clarity: Having a clear understanding of where your money is going can help you make better financial decisions.

Zero-based budgeting is a great way to take control of your finances. If you'd like, I can help you set up a zero-based budget for your specific situation. How does that sound?

Envelope System

Break Down:

ENVELOPE SYSTEM

Set aside cash for specific categories, like groceries or entertainment, in physical envelopes. Once the envelope is empty, you stop spending in that category for the month.

The envelope system is a popular cash-based budgeting technique. It's a hands-on way to control your spending by using physical envelopes to separate your money into different categories. The method works well for people who want a more tactile way to manage their finances and curb overspending. Here's how you can implement it:

How the Envelope System Works:

- Set Your Budget Categories: Decide which categories you want to set aside cash for. **Common ones include:**
  - Groceries
  - Entertainment
  - Dining out
  - Transportation
  - Personal spending
  - Clothing, etc.

- Allocate the Cash: At the beginning of the month (or week, depending on your preference), withdraw cash from your bank account and divide it into separate envelopes, each labeled with the name of the category.
-

For example:

- $400 for groceries
- $100 for entertainment
- $50 for dining out
- $75 for transportation

- Spend from the Envelopes: Use the cash from the corresponding envelope whenever you spend in that category. Once the cash in an envelope is gone, you're done spending in that category for the month (or until the next budgeting period).
- Stop When the Envelope is Empty: The key rule of the envelope system is that once an envelope is empty, you cannot spend any more money in that category. This helps you stay within your limits and avoid impulse purchases.

Benefits of the Envelope System:

- Limits overspending: It forces you to live within your means by giving you a physical limitation on spending.
- Helps with discipline: Knowing that once the money is gone, you can't spend more makes you think twice about your purchases.
- Simple to track: It's easy to see how much you've spent and how much you have left in each category.

Some Tips:

- Cash withdrawals: Make sure you only withdraw the amount you're comfortable spending. If you don't want to carry around large amounts of cash, you can use smaller amounts for categories you tend to overspend on.
- Modify categories as needed: You can adjust your categories each month, depending on your needs. For example, if you're saving for a vacation, you might have an envelope for that and put money into it every month.
- Digital Alternatives: If you don't want to use physical cash, there are digital versions of this system using apps like GoodBudget or Mvelopes where you can create envelopes in your phone to track expenses without the physical cash.

If you're curious, I can help you come up with a basic envelope breakdown for your budget. How do you feel about using cash for your spending categories? Would you like suggestions for what categories to focus on?

Consistency is Key to Your Budget Without Feeling Deprived

Budgeting isn't about denying yourself enjoyment or fun—it's about making intentional choices that align with your goals and values. When you prioritize what matters most to you, you can strike a healthy balance between financial discipline and treating yourself. Here's how you can approach budgeting in a way that allows for fun while keeping your financial goals on track:

KEY TAKEAWAYS

Budgeting empowers you to take control of your money. By creating a plan, you can reduce stress, avoid debt, and work toward your financial goals. Choose a budgeting method that resonates with you, and don't be afraid to tweak it as you go.

ACTION STEPS TO TAKE NOW:

- Write down your monthly income after taxes.
- Categorize your expenses and assign amounts to each category.
- Select a budgeting method and try it for the next month.
- Review your budget weekly to track progress and make adjustments.

When you prioritize what matters most to you, you can strike a healthy balance between financial discipline and treating yourself. Here's how you can approach budgeting in a way that allows for fun while keeping your financial goals on track:

1. **Plan for a "Fun Fund":**
Rather than letting impulse shopping or spontaneous spending derail your budget, you can allocate a specific portion of your monthly income to a "fun fund." This allows you to spend guilt-free on activities you enjoy, such as:

- Going out for dinner
- Buying something you've been eyeing
- Taking a small trip or enjoying entertainment By planning for this, you can enjoy these things without feeling bad about it, because you've already accounted for them in your budget.

2. **Set Clear Priorities:**
Think about what truly brings you joy or value. Maybe it's travel, hobbies, or going out with friends. By clearly identifying your priorities, you can allocate your funds more mindfully. For example, if traveling is a priority, you can reduce spending in other categories, like dining out, to save up for trips.

3. **Budgeting is a Dynamic Process:**
Your life circumstances, goals, and priorities will change over time, and so should your budget. A budget isn't static—it's a living document that should adapt to your evolving needs. Here's how to keep it flexible:

- Review regularly: Make it a habit to check in on your budget weekly or monthly. Are you on track to meet your goals? Do you need to adjust spending in any areas?
- Adapt to life changes: Whether you're getting a raise, experiencing a significant life event (like moving or starting a family), or shifting your financial goals, adjust your budget accordingly.
- Celebrate wins: When you hit a savings goal or stick to your budget for the month, take time to celebrate those small victories. You've worked hard, and it's important to acknowledge your progress.

4. **Avoid the "All-or-Nothing" Mindset:**
Sometimes, people think that budgeting means cutting out everything fun. But it's really about balance. You can still enjoy life while being financially responsible. The key is mindful spending: Make conscious decisions about what's worth spending on, and when you do, make it count. It's the small, intentional pleasures that often bring the most satisfaction.

5. **Use Budgeting Tools to Stay On Track:**
There are plenty of budgeting apps and tools that can help you manage your spending while ensuring you have enough for both your needs and wants. Apps like Mint, YNAB (You Need a Budget), or GoodBudget can help you allocate funds to different categories, track your spending, and make adjustments as needed.

Example of a Balanced Monthly Budget:
Let's say you have $3,000 in income for the month. Here's an example of how you might structure your budget, incorporating both essentials and some fun:

- 50% for Needs (Essentials): $1,500
  - Rent, utilities, groceries, insurance, transportation, etc.
- 30% for Wants (Fun & Lifestyle): $900
  - Fun fund: $200
  - Dining out and entertainment: $300
  - Hobbies or travel fund: $400
- 20% for Savings/Debt Repayment: $600
  - Emergency funds, retirement savings, or paying off debt.

In this setup, you still have plenty of room for fun and enjoyment while ensuring your basic needs are covered and you're saving for the future.

Budgeting isn't about deprivation it's about mindful spending and ensuring your money supports your goals and values. By prioritizing what's most important to you and regularly revisiting your budget, you can enjoy life while also securing your financial future.

How do you feel about creating a balance between fun and financial responsibility in your budget? Would you like help setting up a budget like this or brainstorming some "fun fund" ideas?

Expense Tracker

MONTH: ______

INCOME

DESCRIPTION	GROSS AMOUNT	AFTER TAX
SOURCE 1:		
SOURCE 2:		
OTHERS:		
TOTAL		

FIXED EXPENSES

DATE	DESCRIPTION	AMOUNT
	TOTAL	

VARIABLE EXPENSES

DATE	DESCRIPTION	AMOUNT
	TOTAL	

	BUDGET	ACTUAL	DIFFERENCE
TOTAL INCOME			
TOTAL EXPENSES			
TOTAL SAVINGS			
DEBT PAYOFF			
NET BALANCE			

PERSONAL FINANCE

LEARN TO MASTER YOUR MONEY & IMPROVE YOUR LIFE

CHAPTER 03

FUTURE PLANNING

CHAPTER 03

SAVING FOR THE FUTURE

"Secure Your Tomorrow, Today!"

Saving money is so much more than just putting away extra cash; it's an essential part of taking control of your financial future and ensuring you have the resources you need to achieve your goals and weather any unexpected storms. By being intentional about saving, you open up opportunities and create a financial safety net that can give you peace of mind and freedom.

The Importance of an Emergency Fund

Life is unpredictable. An emergency fund acts as a safety net, covering unexpected expenses like medical bills, car repairs, or sudden job loss. Without it, these emergencies can spiral into debt.

Experts recommend saving at least three to six months' worth of living expenses. If that feels overwhelming, start small and aim for $500 to $1,000 as your initial goal. Once you've reached that milestone, continue building over time.

PRO TIP

Keep your emergency fund in a separate high-yield savings account to earn interest while ensuring the money is easily accessible when needed.

Short-Term vs. Long-Term Savings Goals

Not all savings goals are created equal. Divide your goals into short-term and long-term to make them more manageable.

SHORT-TERM GOALS (1–5 YEARS):

- A vacation
- A new car
- Holiday gifts
- Starting a side hustle

LONG-TERM GOALS (5+ YEARS):

- Buying a home
- Children's education
- Retirement

For short-term goals, consider keeping your money in a regular savings account. For long-term goals, explore investment options like mutual funds or retirement accounts to grow your money over time.

By being intentional about saving, you open up opportunities and create a financial safety net that can give you peace of mind and freedom.

1. Building an Emergency Fund:

One of the most important savings goals is building an emergency fund. This fund is designed to cover unexpected expenses, like medical bills, car repairs, or a job loss. Ideally, you want to save enough to cover 3 to 6 months' worth of living expenses. Having this cushion ensures you don't have to rely on credit cards or loans in times of crisis, and it gives you the financial confidence to handle life's surprises.

- Start small: If saving a few months' worth of expenses feels overwhelming, start with a smaller goal—maybe $500 or $1,000—and build from there.
- Automate your savings: Set up automatic transfers to a dedicated savings account, so you consistently contribute, even if it's a small amount each month.

2. Saving for Big Life Goals (Like a Dream Vacation):

Saving for specific life experiences or goals, like a dream vacation, a wedding, or buying a home, can be incredibly motivating. When you set aside money for something meaningful, it makes the process more exciting and gives you a tangible reason to save.

- Break it down: Start by estimating how much you need for the goal (e.g., a vacation might cost $5,000). Then break it down into manageable chunks (e.g., saving $200/month for 25 months).
- Use a separate account: Set up a separate savings account for your goal. It makes it easier to track your progress and helps avoid spending money on something else.

3. Investing for Retirement:

Saving for retirement is a proactive step toward financial freedom. The earlier you start, the more time your money has to grow thanks to the power of compound interest. Whether through employer-sponsored plans like a 401(k) or personal accounts like an IRA, contributing to retirement savings regularly ensures that you're not left scrambling when you're ready to stop working.

- Take advantage of employer contributions: If your employer offers a retirement match (like a 401(k) match), try to contribute at least enough to get the full match—it's essentially free money.
- Investing over saving: While saving is important, investing in stocks, bonds, or other assets allows your money to grow over time and keep up with inflation.

4. Creating Opportunities Through Saving:

When you save intentionally, you create flexibility in your life. You can take advantage of opportunities that arise, such as:

- Starting a side business
- Taking a career break for personal development
- Seizing investment opportunities
- Buying a house or property when the right moment comes

By saving, you're not just protecting yourself from the unexpected; you're also positioning yourself to take advantage of the opportunities that align with your personal and financial goals.

5. Saving for Financial Freedom:

Ultimately, saving money is about achieving financial independence the freedom to make decisions based on what you truly want, not out of financial necessity. When you have savings in place, whether it's for emergencies, opportunities, or long-term goals, you're less reliant on external factors (like work or debt) and more in control of your financial destiny.

Actionable Steps for Effective Saving:

- Set clear goals: Whether it's building an emergency fund, saving for a vacation, or investing for retirement, knowing why you're saving helps you stay motivated.
- Automate your savings: Set up automatic transfers to savings or investment accounts so you don't even have to think about it.
- Track your progress: Regularly check in on your goals to make sure you're on track, and adjust as necessary.
- Start small, but start now: Even if you can only save a small amount initially, the key is to start. As your income increases, try to increase your savings rate.

Saving money is about being proactive, not reactive. It's about creating a solid foundation for your future while giving yourself the freedom to live and enjoy life today. Whether you're saving for the unexpected or a big dream, each step you take brings you closer to financial security and personal opportunity.

Are you currently saving for any specific goals? I'd love to help you break them down and create a plan if you'd like!

How to Save More Effectively

Saving doesn't mean you need to sacrifice your quality of life. Here are practical strategies to build your savings without feeling deprived:

- **Automate Your Savings:** Set up automatic transfers from your checking account to your savings account every payday. Paying yourself first ensures your savings grow consistently.
- **Cut Back on Non-Essentials:** Identify areas where you can reduce spending, like dining out, subscriptions, or impulse shopping, and redirect those funds to your savings.
- **Embrace the 30-Day Rule:** Before making a non-essential purchase, wait 30 days. This cooling-off period helps curb impulsive spending.
- **Take Advantage of Windfalls:** Use tax refunds, bonuses, or unexpected income to boost your savings.

Saving Challenges to Keep You Motivated

Turn saving into a game with challenges that make the process fun and rewarding:

- **The 52-Week Challenge:** Save $1 the first week, $2 the second week, and so on until you've saved $1,378 by the end of the year.
- **The No-Spend Challenge:** Pick a week or month where you only spend money on essentials.

Where to Keep Your Savings

Choosing the right place to store your savings can help your money grow faster:

- **High-Yield Savings Accounts:** Offer higher interest rates than traditional savings accounts.
- **Certificates of Deposit (CDs):** Lock your money away for a set term in exchange for a higher interest rate. Ideal for long-term goals.
- **Money Market Accounts:** Combine features of savings and checking accounts, offering higher interest rates and limited access to funds.

Saving Challenges to Keep You Motivated

The 52-Week Challenge

- In the 52-Week Challenge, you save an increasing amount each week. Starting with $1 in week one, and increasing the amount by $1 every week, by the end of the year, you'll have saved $1,378. The beauty of this challenge is that it's gradual, so the increases aren't overwhelming.

- Here's a simple breakdown of the savings:
- **Week 1:** Save $1
- **Week 2:** Save $2
- **Week 3:** Save $3
- And so on, until...
- **Week 52:** Save $52
- At the end of 52 weeks, you will have saved a total of $1,378.

- One option for success with this challenge is to future plan. Some people like to start by saving larger amounts in the first few weeks when they have more flexibility, and then adjust if necessary later in the year.

The No-Spend Challenge

In the No-Spend Challenge, you choose a set time period—whether it's a week or a whole month—during which you only spend money on essentials, like food, utilities, and necessary transportation. This helps to curb impulse spending, reset spending habits, and focus on what's truly necessary.

Some tips for a successful No-Spend Challenge:

- **Plan meals:** Avoid take-out or eating out by meal prepping and using what you already have in your pantry.
- **Cut back on subscriptions:** Pause any unnecessary subscription services (e.g., streaming services, magazines, or apps).
- **Get creative with entertainment:** Instead of spending money on activities, explore free events or enjoy hobbies that don't cost anything (e.g., reading, hiking, or working on DIY projects).
- **Track your progress:** This can help keep you motivated and accountable.

Both challenges focus on mindful spending and saving, and they can be powerful tools for improving your finances.

KEY TAKEAWAYS

- Begin with manageable savings goals—every dollar adds up.
- Create an emergency fund to shield yourself from unexpected expenses.
- Break your goals into short-term and long-term categories to stay organized and on track.
- Set up automatic savings and participate in challenges to keep yourself motivated.

ACTION STEPS TO TAKE NOW:

- Choose your first savings goal, such as an emergency fund, vacation, or new car.
- Open a high-yield savings account to help your emergency fund grow faster.
- Set up an automatic transfer to your savings account on payday.
- Select a savings challenge to keep the process enjoyable and motivating.

CHAPTER 04

OWN YOUR DEBT AND LEARN TO MANAGE IT

CHAPTER 04

OWN YOUR DEBT AND LEARN TO MANAGE IT

"Own Your Debt, Realize it Doesn't Own You"

Debt can be a helpful tool when used wisely, allowing us to make important purchases like a home or education. However, when it's not managed carefully, it can quickly become overwhelming. This chapter aims to gently guide you through understanding the different types of debt, offering practical strategies to manage it in a healthy way, and helping you take steps toward a more secure and balanced financial future.

Types of Debt: The Good, the Bad, and the Workable

Not all debt is created equal. Recognizing the types of debt you have can help you create a plan to control it.

- **Good Debt:** Often viewed as an investment in your future, good debt includes things like mortgages, student loans, or small business loans. These types of debt can help build wealth or increase your earning potential over time when managed well.
- **Bad Debt:** High-interest debt, such as credit card balances or payday loans, can quickly become overwhelming if not addressed in time. It's important to stay mindful of these debts to avoid them spiraling out of control.
- **Neutral Debt:** Some debt, like car loans, falls in between good and bad. Whether it's beneficial or not often depends on the interest rates and repayment terms, so it's important to understand the details before committing.

WHY PEOPLE STRUGGLE WITH DEBT

Debt challenges often arise from unexpected circumstances, like medical emergencies or job loss, but they can also stem from overspending or lack of financial education. Acknowledging how debt happens is the first step toward taking control. Understanding that challenges can help create a more compassionate perspective on debt, reminding us that financial struggles are often not a matter of irresponsibility, but a complex mix of circumstances and decisions. Working toward managing and reducing debt is a journey that requires patience, support, and sometimes a fresh start.

Interventions for Paying Off Debt

Approaching debt requires a clear plan. Here are two popular approaches:

THE SNOWBALL METHOD

- Focus on paying off your smallest debts first while making minimum payments on larger ones.
- As each small debt is paid off, roll that payment into the next debt.
- This method builds momentum and motivation.

THE AVALANCHE METHOD

- Focus on paying off debts with the highest interest rates first.
- This approach saves more money in the long run but may take longer to see progress.
- Consistency is the key.

Choose the method that aligns with your ability and financial goals.

Negotiating and Refinancing

Sometimes, you can lower the cost of your debt through negotiation or refinancing.

- Call debt-holder companies and ask for a lower interest rate, especially if you have a good payment history.
- Consider consolidating high-interest debt into a lower-interest personal loan or balance transfer credit card.
- Refinance student loans or mortgages to lock in better rates.

These strategies can save you money and make payments more manageable.

Building a Debt Repayment Plan

Create a plan that fits your budget and keeps you accountable. Start by listing all your debts, including:

- Creditor name
- Total balance
- Interest rate
- Minimum monthly payment
- Number/years of payments

Then allocate extra funds each month to the debt you're focusing on, whether using the snowball or avalanche method.

The Snow Ball Method

The Snowball Method is a popular debt repayment strategy that focuses on paying off your smallest debts first and gradually working your way up to larger ones. The idea is that by knocking out the smaller debts quickly, you'll gain a sense of accomplishment and momentum, which can help you stay motivated as you tackle bigger debts.

How the Snowball Method works:

1. **List Your Debts:** Write down all of your debts, from smallest to largest. Don't worry about interest rates for this method; the focus is on the amount owed.
2. **Make Minimum Payments:** For every debt except the smallest one, continue making only the minimum payments. This ensures that you're not neglecting any debt, while still focusing your efforts on the smallest one.
3. **Pay Extra on the Smallest Debt:** Put any extra money you have toward paying off the smallest debt. The idea is to pay it off as quickly as possible, which helps you feel a sense of achievement and clears one debt from your list.
4. **Move to the Next Debt:** Once the smallest debt is paid off, take the amount you were paying on that debt and apply it to the next smallest debt, while continuing to make minimum payments on the others. This creates a "snowball" effect, where the amount you're paying toward the next debt keeps growing as you eliminate smaller debts.
5. **Repeat:** Keep moving down your list of debts, paying them off one by one, until they're all gone.

Why the Snowball Method Works

- **Psychological Boost:** Paying off smaller debts first gives you quick wins, which can be incredibly motivating. It helps you build momentum and stay engaged in the process.
- **Simplicity:** This method is straightforward and easy to follow. You don't have to worry about complicated calculations or interest rates—just focus on clearing debts one at a time.
- **Emotional Satisfaction:** The sense of relief and progress from crossing off debt can keep you committed to the goal of becoming debt-free.

Potential Drawbacks

While the Snowball Method can be very motivating, it's not always the most cost-effective approach. If your larger debts have higher interest rates, you could end up paying more in interest over time compared to other methods, like the Avalanche Method (which focuses on paying off debts with the highest interest rates first).

However, many people find that the emotional payoff of the Snowball Method helps them stay on track, even if it might cost a bit more in the long run. Ultimately, it's about what keeps you motivated and moving forward toward becoming debt-free.

The Avalance Method

The Avalanche Method is another effective debt repayment strategy, but it focuses on paying off your debts based on interest rates, rather than the size of the balances. This method can save you money in the long run by reducing the amount of interest you pay over time.

How the Avalanche Method works:

1. **List Your Debts:** Write down all your debts, including credit cards, loans, and any other outstanding balances, from the one with the highest interest rate to the lowest.
2. **Make Minimum Payments:** For every debt, continue making the minimum payments, just like with the Snowball Method. This ensures you're not falling behind on any accounts.
3. **Pay Extra on the Highest Interest Debt:** Focus all your extra money toward paying off the debt with the highest interest rate first. This will reduce the amount of interest you pay over time and help you pay off the debt faster.
4. **Move to the Next Debt:** Once the debt with the highest interest rate is paid off, take the money you were putting toward it and apply it to the debt with the next highest interest rate, while continuing to make minimum payments on the others.
5. **Repeat:** Keep tackling the highest-interest debt remaining on your list until all your debts are paid off.

Why the Avalanche Method Works

- **Save Money on Interest:** By paying off the debts with the highest interest rates first, you reduce the overall interest you pay over time. This can save you a significant amount of money, especially with high-interest debts like credit cards.
- **Faster Debt Repayment:** Because you're tackling the most expensive debt first, you'll pay off your debts faster than you would with the Snowball Method, which can help you become debt-free sooner.

Potential Drawbacks

- Slower Wins: The biggest challenge with the Avalanche Method is that it may take longer to see progress. If your highest-interest debt has a large balance, you might not pay it off right away, which can be discouraging for some people. Unlike the Snowball Method, where small debts are paid off quickly, the Avalanche Method doesn't offer the same psychological boosts.
- **Requires Patience:** Since the focus is on the interest rate rather than the balance size, it can feel less rewarding at times. However, the long-term financial benefits can be significant.

Who the Avalanche Method is Best For:
The Avalanche Method works best for those who are motivated by the financial benefit of reducing interest payments. If you're focused on saving money and are comfortable with the idea of slower, but more strategic, progress, this method can be an excellent choice.
Both the Snowball and Avalanche methods can help you get out of debt, but choosing the right one depends on your financial situation and what will keep you motivated on your journey to becoming debt-free.

Negotiating and Refinancing

Negotiating and refinancing are two powerful tools that can help you manage and reduce your debt more effectively. Here's an overview of each approach:

Negotiating Debt

Negotiating your debt means working with your creditors to potentially lower your payments, reduce your interest rates, or even settle a portion of the debt for less than what you owe. It's especially helpful if you're struggling to make payments or facing financial hardship.

How to negotiate your debt:

1. **Contact Your Creditors:** The first step is reaching out to your creditors (credit card companies, loan servicers, etc.). Be honest about your financial situation. Many companies are willing to work with you if they know you're trying to pay off your debt.
2. **Explain Your Situation:** Let them know why you're having trouble making payments (e.g., job loss, medical emergencies, etc.). Be polite but firm, and explain that you want to find a solution that works for both sides.
3. **Request Lower Interest Rates:** Ask if they can reduce your interest rates, which can lower your monthly payments and help you pay off your debt faster. Some creditors may be willing to offer a temporary reduction in rates or work out a payment plan.
4. **Ask About Settling the Debt:** In some cases, creditors may agree to a "settlement" where you pay a lump sum that's less than what you owe. This can be helpful if you're unable to pay off the full amount, but keep in mind that it may impact your credit score.
5. **Get Everything in Writing:** If you reach an agreement, make sure to get the terms in writing. This protects you and ensures that both parties are clear about the arrangement.

Refinancing

Refinancing involves replacing an existing loan or debt with a new one, usually with better terms such as a lower interest rate or longer repayment period. Refinancing can be a great way to reduce your monthly payments or save money on interest, especially if your credit has improved or interest rates have dropped since you first took out the loan.

How refinancing works:

1. **Assess Your Current Debt:** Before refinancing, evaluate your current loans or credit card balances. Look at your interest rates, monthly payments, and remaining balances. Refinancing is most beneficial when you can secure a lower interest rate or better terms.
2. **Shop Around for Better Rates:** When you refinance, it's essential to shop around for the best deal. Check with banks, credit unions, and online lenders to compare rates and terms. Make sure to check the fees associated with refinancing (e.g., origination fees, closing costs) to determine if it's financially worthwhile.
3. **Consider the Terms:** When refinancing, you may be able to extend your loan term, which can reduce your monthly payments. However, keep in mind that while this lowers your monthly obligations, it can also result in paying more interest over time.
4. **Apply for Refinancing:** Once you've found a lender and terms that work for you, apply for refinancing. The new loan will pay off your existing debt, and you'll start making payments on the new loan with the updated terms.
5. **Understand the Impact on Your Credit:** Refinancing can affect your credit score. When you apply for refinancing, it may result in a hard inquiry on your credit report. However, if you refinance to a lower interest rate and make timely payments, it can improve your score over time.

When to Consider Negotiating or Refinancing

- **Negotiating** is a good option if you're struggling to make payments, have high interest rates, or are facing temporary financial difficulties. It can provide immediate relief without adding new debt.
- **Refinancing** is ideal if you've built up equity (in the case of mortgages or car loans) or have a better credit score than when you originally took out the loan. It can help reduce interest rates and lower monthly payments.

Both strategies can provide relief, and sometimes you might even use a combination of both. Negotiating can help with short-term struggles, while refinancing can be a more permanent solution if you qualify for better loan terms. Always make sure to assess the pros and cons and choose the path that best fits your financial goals.

Staying Debt-Free After Repayment

Once you've paid off debt, staying debt-free requires ongoing discipline:

Staying debt-free after repayment requires commitment and consistent effort, but with the right mindset and financial habits, you can continue to build wealth, enjoy financial freedom, and avoid falling back into debt. Remember, it's not about perfection—it's about making smart choices and staying disciplined over time.

WHEN TO SEEK PROFESSIONAL HELP

If your debt feels overwhelming, don't hesitate to seek assistance. Nonprofit credit counseling agencies can help you create a debt management plan. Avoid for-profit companies that charge high fees for services you can often handle yourself or with a nonprofit agency.

KEY TAKEAWAYS

- Understand the types of debt you have and prioritize repayment based on your financial situation.
- Choose a repayment strategy (snowball or avalanche) that works best for you.
- Negotiate or refinance debt to save money on interest.
- Build an emergency fund to avoid falling back into debt.

ACTION STEPS TO TAKE NOW:

- List all your debts, including balances, interest rates, and minimum payments.
- Choose a repayment strategy and create a plan.
- Set aside time to negotiate lower interest rates or explore refinancing options.
- Commit to a budget that prevents new debt and supports consistent repayment.

Staying debt-free after repayment is a crucial part of achieving long-term financial health and maintaining the freedom you've worked hard to regain. Once you've paid off your debts, it's important to build habits that prevent you from falling back into the same cycle. Here are some strategies to help you stay debt-free:

1. Create and Stick to a Budget

- Track Your Spending: Understand exactly where your money is going each month. A detailed budget can help you prevent overspending and ensure you're saving enough for future needs.
- Follow the 50/30/20 Rule: Allocate 50% of your income to needs (like housing and groceries), 30% to wants (like entertainment and dining out), and 20% to savings and debt repayment. This framework helps you balance your spending and stay financially secure.

2. Build an Emergency Fund

- Save for the Unexpected: Having an emergency fund (typically 3-6 months of living expenses) provides a cushion when life throws unexpected expenses your way, such as medical bills or car repairs. This helps you avoid turning to credit cards or loans in times of need.
- Automate Your Savings: Set up automatic transfers to your savings account each month. This ensures that you're consistently building your emergency fund without having to think about it.

3. Live Within Your Means

- Avoid Lifestyle Inflation: As your income increases, it's tempting to upgrade your lifestyle—buying a bigger house, a new car, or more expensive clothing. While it's important to enjoy life, it's also crucial to avoid letting your spending grow with your income.
- Prioritize Needs Over Wants: Focus on spending money on essential needs first, and be mindful of your wants. Limiting impulse purchases can help you stay within your budget and avoid unnecessary debt.

4. Use Credit Wisely

- Pay Off Credit Cards in Full: Avoid carrying balances from month to month. If you have a credit card, always try to pay the full balance by the due date to avoid interest charges and debt accumulation.
- Be Cautious with New Debt: While having a credit card or taking on debt isn't inherently bad, always be mindful of your ability to repay it. Only borrow what you can comfortably pay back and avoid unnecessary loans.

5. Maintain a Healthy Relationship with Money

- Set Financial Goals: Having clear, specific goals (like saving for retirement or a vacation) helps you stay focused on the bigger picture. These goals can give you a sense of purpose and direction when it comes to managing money.
- Revisit Your Budget Regularly: Life changes, and so do your financial needs. Periodically reassess your budget and financial goals to ensure you're on track and adjusting for any changes in your income or expenses.

6. Invest for the Future

- Contribute to Retirement Accounts: Once you're debt-free, make it a priority to contribute to retirement savings accounts like a 401(k) or IRA. This ensures you're setting yourself up for long-term financial security.
- Invest in Yourself: Consider investing in personal growth—whether through education, skill development, or improving your health. These types of investments can increase your earning potential and provide greater financial stability.

7. Avoid Unnecessary Loans

- Avoid Payday and High-Interest Loans: These types of loans can trap you in a cycle of debt due to their high interest rates. If you need to borrow money, look for options that offer lower rates and more manageable terms.
- Plan for Big Purchases: Instead of financing a big purchase, like a new car or a vacation, save up for it in advance. This way, you can pay in full without going into debt.

8. Monitor Your Credit

- Check Your Credit Report: Regularly monitor your credit report to ensure that there are no errors or fraudulent activities. It also helps you stay on top of your credit health and understand how you're doing financially.
- Maintain a Good Credit Score: A good credit score can help you get favorable loan terms when you need them, so paying bills on time and keeping your credit utilization low is essential.

9. Practice Financial Discipline

- Avoid Impulse Purchases: When you feel the urge to make an unplanned purchase, take a moment to reflect on whether it aligns with your financial goals. Implement strategies like waiting 24 hours before buying to curb impulse spending.
- Be Patient and Disciplined: Financial success takes time and effort. Stay committed to your goals and remain disciplined with your spending and saving habits.

10. Surround Yourself with Support

- Find Accountability Partners: Talk about your financial goals with trusted friends or family. They can help keep you accountable and offer advice or support when you need it.
- Learn Continuously: Stay informed about personal finance. There are plenty of books, podcasts, and resources available to help you grow your financial knowledge and make smarter decisions moving forward.

CHAPTER 05

INTRODUCTION TO INVESTING

CHAPTER 05

INTRODUCTION TO INVESTING

"Make the Money, Don't Let it Make You"

Investing can feel overwhelming at first, but it's one of the most rewarding ways to grow your wealth over time. While saving is crucial for immediate needs and emergencies, investing gives your money the chance to grow through the power of compound interest. This chapter is here to walk you through the basics, offering clear explanations and support as you take your first steps toward building an investment portfolio with confidence.

Why Should You Invest?

Investing helps you achieve long-term financial goals, such as:

- Building wealth for retirement.
- Saving for a child's education.
- Have money in case stuff happens
- Generating passive income.

Unlike savings accounts, which often offer minimal interest, investments have the potential to deliver significantly higher returns over time.

The Power of Compound Interest

Compound interest is often called the eighth wonder of the world. It allows your investments to grow exponentially by earning returns not only on your initial investment but also on the returns themselves.

Example:

- You invest $1,000 at a 7% annual return.
- After 1 year, you earn $70 in interest.
- The next year, you earn interest on $1,070.

Over time, this compounding effect can turn small, consistent contributions into a substantial nest egg.

Why Invest?

Investing is one of the most powerful tools for building long-term financial security, but it can feel intimidating. Understanding why you should invest can help you see the bigger picture and give you the confidence to start. Here are some key reasons why investing is important:

1. **Grow Your Wealth**

- Compound Growth: When you invest, your money has the potential to grow over time through compound interest. Essentially, you earn interest on your initial investment, as well as on the interest that accumulates. This "snowball" effect can help your wealth grow exponentially.
- **Higher Returns Than Savings:** While savings accounts are important for short-term goals and emergencies, the interest earned is usually minimal. Investing in stocks, bonds, or other assets can offer higher returns, helping you build wealth faster.

2. **Beat Inflation**

- Protect Against Rising Costs: Inflation erodes the purchasing power of your money over time. If your money is just sitting in a savings account earning low interest, it may lose value in the long run. Investments, especially in assets like stocks or real estate, tend to outpace inflation, helping your wealth grow while maintaining its value.

3. **Plan for Retirement**

- Ensure Financial Freedom: Whether through a 401(k), IRA, or other retirement accounts, investing helps ensure that you have enough money to live comfortably in retirement. The earlier you start, the more time your investments have to grow, allowing you to build a nest egg that supports you later in life.
- **Social Security Isn't Enough:** Relying solely on Social Security benefits may not be enough to maintain your standard of living during retirement. Investing allows you to supplement your retirement savings and have more control over your future.

4. **Achieve Long-Term Goals**

- Funding Big Dreams: Investing can help you save for big life goals, such as buying a home, funding a child's education, or traveling. By putting your money in investments with higher growth potential, you can work toward achieving these goals faster and more efficiently than relying on savings alone.
- Financial Independence: Through consistent investing, you can build the wealth necessary to achieve financial independence—where you no longer need to rely on a paycheck to live comfortably.

5. **Create Passive Income**

- Earnings While You Sleep: Certain types of investments, such as dividend-paying stocks or real estate, can provide a steady stream of passive income. This means you can earn money without actively working for it, giving you more financial flexibility and freedom.

6. **Diversify Your Risk**

- Reduce Risk with Variety: By investing in different types of assets, you can spread out your risk. If one investment performs poorly, others may be doing better, helping to balance out your portfolio. This diversification can reduce the overall risk of losing money and improve the stability of your finances.

7. **Take Control of Your Financial Future**

- Empower Yourself: Investing allows you to have more control over your financial future. Instead of relying solely on external factors like inflation, rising costs, or your employer's retirement plan, investing gives you the ability to shape your financial destiny and work toward financial goals that matter to you.

Investing isn't just for the wealthy it's a tool anyone can use to improve their financial well-being. While it may feel overwhelming at first, getting started with small steps can have a big impact on your future. By investing, you're allowing yourself to build wealth, protect against inflation, and work toward a more secure financial future.

Compound Interest

What is Compound Interest?

Compound interest is often called "interest on interest" because it allows your investment to grow exponentially over time. In simple terms, it means that the interest you earn on your savings or investments is added to your principal balance. From there, you earn interest not just on your initial investment but also on the interest that has already been added. This creates a snowball effect where your money grows at an increasing rate.

Example: If you invest $1,000 at an interest rate of 5% per year, in the first year you would earn $50 in interest (5% of $1,000). In the second year, you would earn interest not just on your original $1,000, but also on the $50 in interest from the previous year. So, you'd earn $52.50 in interest (5% of $1,050), and it continues to grow from there.

Why Do I Need to Know About Compound Interest?

Understanding compound interest is crucial because it can have a huge impact on your financial future. Whether you're saving for retirement, building an emergency fund, or investing for long-term goals, compound interest works to your advantage when you start early and let your investments grow over time.

By starting early, you give your investments more time to benefit from compound interest, allowing your money to grow faster and work harder for you. The longer you leave your investments untouched, the more powerful the effect of compound interest will be. This is why it's often said, "The best time to start investing was yesterday. The second best time is today."

How Does Compound Interest Help or Hurt Me?

How Compound Interest Helps:

1. **Boosts Long-Term Growth:** The longer you leave your money invested, the more it compounds, leading to much larger growth than you'd see with simple interest, where you only earn interest on the initial amount. This is why compound interest is often described as the "eighth wonder of the world"—it helps your money grow faster than you might expect.
2. **Makes Saving Easier:** When you invest or save and let compound interest do the work, you don't have to constantly be adding more money to your account. As long as you continue to make regular contributions and keep your money invested, your returns will continue to grow by themselves.
3. **Helps Build Wealth:** Compound interest is key to building wealth over time, especially for long-term goals like retirement. The more time your money has to compound, the more substantial your returns can be. This can be a game-changer when it comes to financial independence.

How Compound Interest Can Hurt You:

1. **Debt Can Grow Quickly:** Just as compound interest helps your savings grow, it can also work against you if you're in debt. With high-interest loans or credit cards, the interest on your outstanding balance compounds over time, meaning you could end up paying far more than the original amount you borrowed. The longer you carry debt, the more you'll pay due to compounding interest.
2. **Increases Financial Stress:** If you don't manage your debt well, compound interest can make it harder to get ahead financially. For example, if you're only making minimum payments on credit cards or loans, you might only be paying off the interest rather than the principal, causing the balance to grow and making it harder to get out of debt.

3. **The Debt Snowball Effect:** If left unchecked, compound interest on your debt can snowball, meaning the amount you owe increases faster and faster as time goes on, making it harder to catch up. This is why it's critical to pay off high-interest debt quickly.

Why Does It Matter to Me?

Understanding how compound interest works can empower you to make smarter financial decisions. Here's why it's important for both saving and managing debt:

- **For Saving and Investing:** The sooner you start saving or investing, the more you can take advantage of compound interest. Even small contributions early on can grow significantly over time, making compound interest one of the most powerful tools for building wealth.
- **For Managing Debt:** If you have high-interest debt, compound interest can cause your debt to grow faster than you may expect. The longer you carry that debt, the harder it will be to pay off. It's crucial to prioritize paying down high-interest debt as quickly as possible to minimize the damaging effects of compound interest working against you.

In Summary:

- Compound interest is a powerful tool that can work for you by growing your investments over time, but it can also work against you when it comes to debt.
- To benefit from compound interest, focus on starting your investments early and letting them grow.
- To avoid being hurt by compound interest, manage your debt carefully, pay off high-interest loans quickly, and be mindful of credit card balances.

Understanding compound interest gives you the knowledge to make smart financial decisions that can either build wealth or protect you from the pitfalls of debt. It's all about letting time and consistency work in your favor!

Types of Investments

Investing can take many forms. Here are some of the most common options:

STOCKS

Shares of ownership in a company. Stocks have high growth potential but come with higher risk.

ETFS (EXCHANGE-TRADED FUNDS)

Similar to mutual funds but traded like stocks, offering diversification at a lower cost.

BONDS

Loans to governments or corporations that pay interest over time. Bonds are typically lower risk but offer modest returns.

REAL ESTATE

Purchasing property to generate rental income or capital appreciation.

MUTUAL FUNDS

Professionally managed funds that pool money from multiple investors to invest in a mix of stocks, bonds, or other assets.

CRYPTOCURRENCY

Digital currencies like Bitcoin or Ethereum. High risk and volatility but potential for high rewards.

How to Get Started

- **Define Your Goals:** What are you investing for? Retirement? A down payment on a house? Having clear goals will guide your investment choices.
- **Understand Your Risk Tolerance:** How much risk are you willing to take? Younger investors can often afford more risk, while those nearing retirement may prefer safer investments.
- **Start Small:** You don't need a lot of money to begin. Many platforms let you start investing with as little as $5 or $10.
- **Choose an Investment Platform:** Look for beginner-friendly platforms like Robinhood, Acorns, or Vanguard. Research fees and account minimums before committing.

Stock Options: What Are They and How Do They Work?

Stock options can seem complex at first, but understanding them can allow you to enhance your investment strategy. Here's a simplified explanation of stock options, how they work, and what you need to know to make informed decisions.

What Are Stock Options?

Stock options are financial contracts that give you the right, but not the obligation, to buy or sell a stock at a predetermined price (called the strike price) within a specific time frame. There are two main types of stock options:

1. **Call Options:** These give you the right to buy a stock at a specific price within a certain time period. You would buy a call option if you believe the stock price will rise above the strike price.
2. **Put Options**: These give you the right to sell a stock at a specific price within a certain time period. You would buy a put option if you believe the stock price will fall below the strike price.

Key Terms to Know

- **Strike Price:** The price at which you can buy or sell the stock. For a call option, you'll buy the stock at the strike price. For a put option, you'll sell the stock at the strike price.
- **Expiration Date:** The date by which the option must be exercised. After this date, the option expires and becomes worthless.
- **Premium:** The cost of purchasing the option. This is paid upfront when you buy the option.

How Do Stock Options Work?

Let's break it down with an example:

Call Option Example:

- Stock XYZ is trading at $50 per share.
- You buy a call option with a strike price of $55, expiring in one month, for a premium of $2.
- If the stock price goes above $55 (e.g., $60) before the expiration date, you can exercise the option, of buying the stock at $55 and immediately selling it at $60, making a profit.
- Your total profit would be the difference between the selling price ($60) and the strike price ($55), minus the premium you paid ($2). In this case, your profit would be $3 per share ($60 - $55 - $2 = $3).

Put Option Example:

- Stock XYZ is trading at $50 per share.
- You buy a put option with a strike price of $45, expiring in one month, for a premium of $2.
- If the stock price falls below $45 (e.g., to $40), you can exercise the option and sell the stock at $45, making a profit.
- Your total profit would be the difference between the strike price ($45) and the selling price ($40), minus the premium you paid ($2). In this case, your profit would be $3 per share ($45 - $40 - $2 = $3).

Why Do People Use Stock Options?

- Leverage: Stock options allow you to control a larger amount of stock with a smaller initial investment (the premium). This means you can potentially profit from the movement of the stock price without needing to buy or sell the stock outright.
- Hedging: Some investors use stock options as a form of insurance against potential losses in their portfolios. For example, if you own a stock and are concerned that it might decrease in value, you could buy a put option to lock in a sale price, effectively protecting yourself from losses.
- Speculation: Investors might also use stock options to bet on the direction of a stock's price movement. If they believe a stock will rise, they might buy a call option; if they believe it will fall, they might buy a put option. The potential profits can be large if their predictions are correct.

Risks of Stock Options

While stock options can provide high rewards, they also come with significant risks. Here are some things to keep in mind:

- Limited Time: Options have expiration dates. If you don't exercise the option by the expiration date, it becomes worthless, and you lose the premium you paid for it.
- Premium Loss: If the stock price doesn't move in the direction you anticipated, you can lose the entire premium you paid for the option. For example, if the stock price never rises above the strike price of your call option, the option expires worthless, and you lose the premium you paid.
- Complexity: Stock options can be complicated, especially for beginners. Without a good understanding of how options work, you could potentially lose more money than you expected.
- Potential to Lose More Than You Invest: If you are writing (selling) options, you can face unlimited risk. For example, if you sell a call option and the stock price rises far above the strike price, you could be forced to sell the stock at a much lower price than the market value, leading to significant losses.

When to Use Stock Options

- As a Speculative Tool: If you believe a stock will move dramatically in a certain direction, options allow you to profit from this price movement without owning the stock itself.
- For Hedging: If you want to protect a portfolio against potential declines in value, options can provide a safety net by locking in selling prices.
- To Generate Income: Some investors sell options to collect premiums, especially in strategies like covered calls. However, this also comes with risk, especially if the stock moves against the seller.

Stock options can be a powerful financial tool, but they come with both great potential and significant risk. They are not suitable for everyone, and it's essential to have a solid understanding of how they work before incorporating them into your investment strategy. If you're just starting, consider consulting a financial advisor or practicing with a simulated account to get more comfortable with options trading.

By understanding the basics of stock options and their risks and rewards, you can make more informed decisions about whether they fit into your investment plan.

What Are Bonds?

Bonds are a type of investment where you lend money to a government, municipality, or corporation in exchange for periodic interest payments, and the return of your principal at a later date (called the maturity date). In essence, a bond is a loan, but instead of lending money to a person or business directly, you're lending it to an organization that promises to pay you back with interest.

How Do Bonds Work?

When you buy a bond, you are essentially the lender. Here's a breakdown of how they work:

- **Issuing Entity:** A government (local, state, or national) or a company issues a bond to raise money for various projects or activities, like building infrastructure or expanding their business operations.
- **Face Value (Principal):** The face value of a bond is the amount of money you lend to the issuer. For example, if you buy a $1,000 bond, the issuer promises to repay you $1,000 at maturity.
- **Coupon Rate:** This is the interest rate the issuer agrees to pay you for lending them the money. For example, if the bond has a coupon rate of 5%, you would receive $50 annually for each $1,000 bond you hold.
- **Maturity Date:** The maturity date is when the bond issuer will return your principal (the face value) back to you. Bonds can have various maturities, ranging from a few months to several decades.
- **Interest Payments:** Bonds typically pay interest to the bondholder (you) either annually or semi-annually. This is called the coupon payment. The amount of interest is based on the coupon rate and the face value of the bond.

Types of Bonds

Government Bonds:

- These are issued by national governments (such as U.S. Treasury bonds). They are considered very safe because governments are less likely to default.

Examples: U.S. Treasury Bonds, and Municipal Bonds (issued by state or local governments).

Corporate Bonds:

- Issued by companies to raise capital. These bonds tend to offer higher interest rates compared to government bonds because there's more risk involved (companies can default, whereas governments are less likely to).

Examples: Bonds issued by corporations like Apple, Tesla, or Walmart.

Municipal Bonds:

- Issued by state or local governments to fund public projects like schools, hospitals, and highways. These bonds may come with tax advantages, like being exempt from federal taxes.

Example: A city issuing bonds to finance a new subway system.

High-Yield Bonds (Junk Bonds):

- These are bonds issued by companies with lower credit ratings, meaning there is a higher risk that they might default on the loan. To compensate for the higher risk, these bonds offer higher interest rates.

Examples: Bonds from smaller companies or those with a less-than-ideal credit rating.

Why Should You Consider Bonds?

Stability and Predictable Income:

- Bonds are typically less volatile than stocks, providing a more stable source of income. The interest payments offer a regular income stream, which can be appealing for conservative investors or those in retirement.

Diversification:

- Including bonds in your portfolio can help balance risk. Since bonds generally don't move in the same direction as stocks, they can offset losses when the stock market is down.

Safety:

- Government bonds, especially those from stable economies like the U.S., are considered some of the safest investments because governments are less likely to default on their debt

Capital Preservation:

- Bonds return your principal at the maturity date, so if you hold a bond until maturity, you should get your original investment back, barring any defaults.

Risks of Investing in Bonds

Interest Rate Risk:

- The value of bonds is inversely related to interest rates. When interest rates rise, the value of existing bonds falls. This happens because new bonds are issued with higher interest rates, making older bonds with lower rates less attractive.

Credit Risk:

- If the issuer of the bond (whether a government or corporation) experiences financial trouble, they may default on the bond, meaning you may not receive the interest payments or the return of your principal.

Inflation Risk:

- If inflation rises, the fixed interest payments from bonds may not keep up with the rising cost of living, which can erode the purchasing power of your bond income.

Liquidity Risk:

Some bonds may not be easy to sell before their maturity date. If you need to cash out early, you may have to sell your bond at a lower price than you paid for it, especially if interest rates have risen or the issuer's financial situation has worsened.

Bond Prices and Yields

- **Bond Price:** The price of a bond fluctuates in the market based on interest rates and the financial health of the issuer. If a bond's price falls below its face value, it's said to be "trading at a discount"; if it's above face value, it's "trading at a premium."
- **Yield:** The yield on a bond is the return you can expect based on its price and coupon rate. If you buy a bond at face value, the yield will be the coupon rate. However, if you buy a bond at a discount or premium, the yield will adjust accordingly.

Should You Invest in Bonds?

- Bonds can be a great investment choice depending on your financial goals, risk tolerance, and time horizon. They offer stability, and regular income, and are a great way to diversify your investment portfolio. However, they come with risks, particularly interest rate and credit risk, which should be carefully considered. If you're looking for a steady income stream or a safer investment compared to stocks, bonds might be a suitable choice for you.
- If you are new to bonds or uncertain about which type is best for your situation, consider consulting a financial advisor who can help guide you in choosing the right bonds for your portfolio.

By understanding the basics of stock options and their risks and rewards, you can make more informed decisions about whether they fit into your investment plan.

What Are ETFs (Exchange-Traded Funds)?

An Exchange-Traded Fund (ETF) is an investment fund that holds a collection of assets, such as stocks, bonds, commodities, or other securities, and can be bought and sold on a stock exchange, similar to individual stocks. They are designed to offer investors an easy way to diversify their portfolios by investing in a broad range of assets in one trade.

How Do ETFs Work?

ETFs pool investors' money to invest in a diverse portfolio of assets, which could include hundreds or even thousands of stocks or bonds. When you invest in an ETF, you're essentially buying a share of that diversified portfolio.

- **Buying & Selling:** Just like stocks, ETFs can be bought and sold throughout the trading day on a stock exchange. Their prices fluctuate during the day based on the market demand for the ETF and the value of the assets it holds.
- **Structure:** Most ETFs are designed to track the performance of a specific index (such as the S&P 500 or Nasdaq), sector (like technology or healthcare), or asset class (like bonds or commodities). There are also actively managed ETFs, where a team of professionals select the assets to be included in the fund.

Key Characteristics of ETFs

Diversification:

One of the primary benefits of ETFs is that they offer diversification. By holding a wide range of securities in a single ETF, investors gain exposure to multiple assets without having to buy each one individually.

Lower Costs:

ETFs tend to have lower expense ratios compared to mutual funds, because many ETFs are passively managed (i.e., they track an index rather than trying to beat the market). This means you pay less in management fees.

Liquidity:

ETFs are traded on exchanges, and their prices fluctuate throughout the day based on supply and demand. This makes them highly liquid, meaning you can buy or sell your ETF shares at any time during market hours, similar to stocks.

Transparency:
Most ETFs disclose their holdings daily, so you can easily see what assets the fund is invested in. This gives you more transparency compared to other types of investment funds, like mutual funds, which typically disclose holdings less frequently.

Flexibility:
ETFs can be used to track broad indices, specific sectors, or even niche investment strategies. You can choose ETFs that align with your specific investment goals and risk tolerance.

Types of ETFs

Stock ETFs:

- These ETFs invest in a basket of stocks and typically track an index, like the S&P 500 or the Dow Jones Industrial Average. Stock ETFs are great for gaining exposure to the stock market as a whole.

Bond ETFs:

- These ETFs invest in a collection of bonds and can be used to add fixed-income exposure to your portfolio. Bond ETFs can be a good choice for investors seeking more stability and income.

Sector & Industry ETFs:

- These ETFs focus on specific sectors of the economy, such as technology, healthcare, energy, or finance. If you're optimistic about the future performance of a certain industry, you can invest in a sector-specific ETF to gain exposure to that industry.

International ETFs:

- These ETFs invest in companies or bonds from outside the United States, giving you exposure to international markets and allowing you to diversify globally.

Commodity ETFs:

- These ETFs invest in commodities such as gold, oil, or agricultural products. They're useful if you want to gain exposure to commodities without needing to buy physical goods.

Thematic ETFs:

- Thematic ETFs focus on specific themes or trends, such as clean energy, artificial intelligence, or sustainability. These funds can be an exciting way to invest in emerging industries.

Why Should You Invest in ETFs?

Diversification:

1. With just one ETF, you can gain exposure to a wide range of securities, reducing the risk associated with investing in individual stocks or bonds. Diversification helps smooth out the highs and lows of individual investments.

Cost-Effective:

1. ETFs typically have lower fees than mutual funds because they are often passively managed. Lower fees mean you get to keep more of your investment returns.

Liquidity:

1. ETFs are traded on major exchanges, meaning you can buy and sell them throughout the day, just like a stock. This gives you flexibility and liquidity to adjust your portfolio as needed.

Transparency:

1. Most ETFs disclose their holdings daily, giving you a clear picture of where your money is invested.

Flexibility in Strategy:

1. ETFs can fit into various investment strategies. Whether you want broad market exposure, sector-specific investments, or international diversification, there's likely an ETF that aligns with your goals.

Tax Efficiency:

1. ETFs are generally more tax-efficient than mutual funds. When you buy or sell shares in an ETF, you're typically not subject to the capital gains taxes that can arise when mutual funds buy or sell underlying assets within the fund.

Risks of ETFs

Market Risk:

1. Like all investments, ETFs are subject to market fluctuations. The value of your ETF may decrease if the underlying assets (like stocks or bonds) lose value.

Tracking Error:

1. Some ETFs may not perfectly track the index or assets they aim to replicate. This discrepancy is called a tracking error, and it can result in lower returns than the index or asset class the ETF is meant to track.

Liquidity Risk:

- While most ETFs are highly liquid, some niche or specialized ETFs may have lower trading volumes, making it more difficult to buy or sell at your desired price.

Management Fees:

- Although ETFs generally have lower fees than mutual funds, some ETFs—especially actively managed ones—still have management fees that can eat into your returns. Always check the expense ratio before investing.

Sector and Industry Risks:

- If you invest in sector or thematic ETFs, you're more exposed to the risks of that specific sector. For example, investing in a technology ETF means you're highly reliant on the performance of the tech industry.

Should You Invest in ETFs?

ETFs can be a great addition to your investment portfolio, especially if you're looking for a low-cost, diversified, and liquid way to invest. They're particularly useful for long-term investors seeking broad market exposure or specific sector and thematic plays. However, as with any investment, it's important to do your research and understand your goals and risk tolerance.
If you're new to investing, ETFs can be an excellent starting point, providing you with a simple way to build a well-diversified portfolio with minimal effort. If you're more experienced, you can use ETFs strategically to enhance specific parts of your portfolio. As always, consider consulting a financial advisor if you're unsure about how ETFs fit into your overall investment strategy.

What Is Real Estate Investing?

Real estate investing involves purchasing property with the goal of earning a return through rental income, appreciation, or both. It's one of the most popular ways to build wealth, offering opportunities for both long-term growth and steady income.

Real estate can be a physical asset like a house, apartment, or commercial property, or it can be a more indirect investment, such as investing in Real Estate Investment Trusts (REITs), which allow you to invest in real estate without actually owning property.

Types of Real Estate Investments

Residential Real Estate:

- **Single-Family Homes:** This is the most common type of residential property. Investors buy single-family homes, typically rent them out to tenants, and earn rental income.
- **Multi-Family Properties:** These are buildings with multiple units, such as duplexes, triplexes, or apartment complexes. Owning multi-family properties can provide more rental income because there are multiple units generating cash flow.
- **Vacation Rentals**: With platforms like Airbnb and Vrbo, investors can buy homes or apartments and rent them out on a short-term basis, often earning higher rental rates than traditional leases.

Commercial Real Estate:

- **Office Buildings**: Investors buy office space and rent it out to businesses. Office properties are usually leased for longer terms, offering stability but also requiring large capital investments.
- **Retail Properties:** These are shopping centers or standalone stores leased to businesses like restaurants, retailers, or service providers.
- **Industrial Real Estate:** This includes warehouses, factories, or distribution centers. With the growth of e-commerce, industrial real estate has become a highly sought-after investment.

Real Estate Investment Trusts (REITs):

- A REIT is a company that owns and operates income-producing real estate. Investors can buy shares in a REIT just like stocks. It allows you to invest in real estate without having to buy and manage physical property, providing liquidity and a relatively low barrier to entry.

Real Estate Crowdfunding:

- This is a relatively new way to invest in real estate. Through crowdfunding platforms, investors pool their money to finance real estate projects, typically commercial or large residential developments. It allows you to invest with a lower initial amount and diversify your real estate holdings.

Benefits of Real Estate Investing

Cash Flow:

- Rental income is one of the primary ways to earn money from real estate. If you buy a property and rent it out, you can receive regular payments that can help cover expenses and generate profit. The steady cash flow can be especially appealing for those looking for passive income.

Appreciation:

- Over time, real estate values generally increase, allowing your property to appreciate. This can lead to significant profits when you sell the property, especially if the market conditions are favorable.

Tax Benefits:

- Real estate investors often benefit from tax deductions. You can deduct expenses like mortgage interest, property taxes, insurance, maintenance, and depreciation on your property, which can reduce your taxable income.

Leverage:

- Real estate allows you to use leverage, meaning you can borrow money (typically through a mortgage) to buy a property. This means you can control a larger asset with less of your own money. If the property appreciates in value, you can potentially earn a higher return on investment (ROI) than if you used only your own funds.

Inflation Hedge:

- Real estate is often considered a hedge against inflation because property values and rents tend to rise along with inflation. This means your real estate investment may keep pace with the increasing cost of living.

Diversification:

- Real estate provides an opportunity to diversify your investment portfolio. As a non-correlated asset, real estate often moves independently of the stock market, helping to reduce overall portfolio risk.

Risks of Real Estate Investing

Initial Capital Requirement:

Real estate usually requires a significant amount of upfront capital. If you're buying a property, you'll need money for a down payment, closing costs, and potentially repairs or renovations. While some financing options are available, it can still be a barrier for some investors.

Property Management:

Owning physical real estate means dealing with tenants, maintenance, repairs, and property management. If you don't want to manage the property yourself, you may need to hire a property manager, which adds to the cost.

Market Risk:

Real estate markets can fluctuate based on factors like interest rates, the economy, and housing demand. A downturn in the market could lead to lower property values or reduced rental income, which could affect your investment returns.

Illiquidity:

Unlike stocks or bonds, real estate is not a liquid asset. It can take time to sell a property and turn it into cash. This means that if you need to access funds quickly, real estate might not be the best option.

High Costs of Maintenance:

Real estate requires ongoing maintenance and repair costs. Whether it's routine upkeep or dealing with unforeseen issues (such as a broken HVAC or plumbing problems), these expenses can add up and reduce your profitability.

Tenant Risk:

If you are renting out a property, there's always a risk that tenants might not pay rent on time or cause damage to the property. Evicting tenants or dealing with legal issues can be costly and time-consuming.

Real Estate Strategies

Buy and Hold:

This is one of the most common real estate strategies, where investors purchase properties and hold them long-term to benefit from rental income and property appreciation.

Flipping:
Flipping involves buying properties at a lower price, often distressed or in need of repairs, renovating them, and selling them at a higher price for a profit. While potentially lucrative, flipping is often riskier because it requires significant capital and expertise in property renovations.

Wholesaling:
Wholesaling involves finding properties at below-market prices, securing them under contract, and then selling the contract to other investors for a fee. It's a strategy that doesn't require a large upfront investment but can require good networking skills and knowledge of real estate markets.

House Hacking:
House hacking involves purchasing a multi-family property, living in one unit, and renting out the other units to cover your mortgage and generate passive income. It's a popular strategy for beginner real estate investors looking to reduce living expenses and build wealth.

Real Estate Syndications:
Real estate syndications involve pooling money with other investors to purchase large-scale properties (like apartment complexes or commercial buildings). As an investor in a syndication, you get a share of the profits without the responsibility of managing the property.

Should You Invest in Real Estate?

Real estate can be an excellent way to build wealth, but it's not without its challenges. It's important to assess your financial situation, risk tolerance, and goals before diving in. Real estate tends to require significant capital, time, and effort, especially if you are buying physical property.

If you're looking for passive income and the potential for long-term wealth building, real estate could be a great fit. However, if you're seeking more liquid or lower-maintenance investments, it might be better to look at other options like stocks or ETFs.

If you're just starting, you might want to consider indirect real estate investments like REITs or crowdfunding platforms, which allow you to invest in real estate without owning and managing property directly. Alternatively, consulting with a real estate professional can help you navigate the complexities of the market and develop a strategy that aligns with your goals.

What Are Mutual Funds?

A mutual fund is an investment vehicle that pools money from many investors to purchase a diversified portfolio of stocks, bonds, or other securities. Instead of purchasing individual stocks or bonds, investors in a mutual fund own shares of the fund, and the fund's managers use the pooled money to invest in a variety of assets according to the fund's objective.

How Do Mutual Funds Work?

When you invest in a mutual fund, your money is combined with the money of other investors to create a larger pool. The fund is managed by professional fund managers who decide which securities (stocks, bonds, etc.) to buy, hold, and sell based on the fund's strategy.

- NAV (Net Asset Value): The value of a mutual fund share is determined by the net asset value (NAV), which is the total value of the fund's assets minus its liabilities, divided by the number of outstanding shares. The NAV is calculated at the end of each trading day.
- Management: Mutual funds can be actively or passively managed. Actively managed mutual funds have a fund manager or team who make decisions about which assets to buy and sell. In contrast, passively managed funds (like index funds) aim to replicate the performance of a specific market index (e.g., the S&P 500) and require less management.
- Dividends and Capital Gains: Investors in mutual funds may receive income from dividends and interest paid on the underlying securities, as well as capital gains when the fund sells securities at a profit.

Types of Mutual Funds

Equity (Stock) Funds:
These funds invest primarily in stocks and aim to provide high returns by investing in companies with growth potential. They are generally considered riskier than bond funds but offer higher potential rewards.

Bond Funds:
Bond funds invest in bonds or other fixed-income securities. These funds are typically considered safer and provide steady income, but they tend to offer lower returns than equity funds.

Balanced Funds:
These funds invest in both stocks and bonds to provide a balanced mix of growth and income. Balanced funds are designed to offer moderate risk and return, making them suitable for investors looking for a diversified portfolio without high volatility.

Money Market Funds:

Money market funds invest in short-term debt securities, such as Treasury bills or commercial paper, offering low-risk, low-return investments. They are used by investors who are looking for safety and liquidity.

Index Funds:

Index funds are passively managed mutual funds designed to replicate the performance of a specific market index, like the S&P 500 or the Dow Jones Industrial Average. They typically have lower fees than actively managed funds because they don't require as much management.

Target-Date Funds:

These funds are designed for investors who plan to retire at a specific time, such as 2030 or 2050. The fund automatically adjusts its asset allocation over time, becoming more conservative as the target date approaches.

International Funds:

These funds invest in stocks or bonds outside of your home country. International funds are an option for diversifying your portfolio globally and gaining exposure to foreign markets.

Sector Funds:

Sector funds focus on specific industries, such as technology, healthcare, or energy. While they provide concentrated exposure to one sector, they also come with higher risks because of their lack of diversification.

Benefits of Investing in Mutual Funds

Diversification:

Mutual funds allow you to invest in a wide range of assets in a single fund. By owning shares in a mutual fund, you gain exposure to a diversified portfolio without having to buy each security individually. This diversification helps reduce risk.

Professional Management:

Mutual funds are managed by professional fund managers who are experienced in analyzing markets and making investment decisions. For investors who don't have the time or expertise to manage their investments, mutual funds offer an easy way to benefit from professional management.

Accessibility:
Mutual funds typically have relatively low minimum investment requirements, making them accessible to many types of investors, from beginners to experienced ones. You can also invest regularly through systematic investment plans (SIPs), allowing you to invest a fixed amount every month

Liquidity:
Mutual funds are generally liquid investments, meaning you can sell your shares at any time at the current NAV. While there may be fees or penalties for early withdrawals in some cases, most mutual funds allow you to access your money fairly easily.

Automatic Reinvestment:
Many mutual funds offer the option to automatically reinvest any dividends or capital gains back into the fund, which can help grow your investment over time through compounding.

Variety:
There are many different types of mutual funds available, allowing you to choose funds that align with your investment goals, risk tolerance, and time horizon.

Risks of Investing in Mutual Funds

Market Risk:
Like all investments in the stock or bond market, mutual funds are subject to market fluctuations. The value of your mutual fund shares can go up or down depending on the performance of the underlying assets, which can result in a loss of value.

Management Fees:
Mutual funds charge management fees for the professional oversight and management of the fund. These fees are usually expressed as the expense ratio, which can vary significantly between funds. Actively managed funds tend to have higher fees than passively managed funds like index funds.

Performance Risk:
There's no guarantee that the mutual fund will perform well, even with a professional manager at the helm. Past performance is not indicative of future results, and fund managers may make decisions that don't perform as expected.

No Control Over Investments:
When you invest in a mutual fund, you're relying on the fund manager to make the investment decisions. You don't have any control over which individual securities are bought or sold within the fund.

Capital Gains Distributions:

Mutual funds may distribute capital gains to investors if the fund manager has sold securities at a profit. These distributions are taxable, which could result in unexpected tax liabilities even if you didn't sell any shares.

Investment Strategy Risk:

Some mutual funds follow aggressive investment strategies, which may involve taking on higher risks. If the fund manager's strategy doesn't pay off, you could lose money.

Should You Invest in Mutual Funds?

Mutual funds can be a great option for investors looking for diversification, professional management, and a simple way to invest. They are especially suitable for long-term investors who want exposure to a broad range of assets without having to pick individual stocks or bonds. If you're new to investing, mutual funds provide an easy way to get started. Additionally, index funds and target-date funds are good choices for investors who want a low-cost, passive investment strategy.

However, like all investments, mutual funds come with risks. It's important to understand the fund's investment strategy, fees, and performance history before you invest. If you're uncertain about which mutual funds are right for you, consider speaking with a financial advisor who can help you choose the best options based on your financial goals and risk tolerance.

What is Cryptocurrency?

Cryptocurrency is a type of digital or virtual currency that uses cryptography for security. Unlike traditional currencies issued by governments (like the dollar or euro), cryptocurrencies are decentralized and typically operate on a technology called blockchain.

Blockchain is a distributed ledger that records all transactions across a network of computers. It ensures that all transactions are transparent, secure, and immutable (meaning they can't be altered once confirmed). The most well-known cryptocurrency is Bitcoin, but there are thousands of other cryptocurrencies, including Ethereum, Ripple (XRP), Litecoin, and many more.

How Does Cryptocurrency Work?

Decentralized Nature:

- Most cryptocurrencies are decentralized, meaning they are not controlled by a central authority like a government or a bank. Instead, they are maintained by a network of computers (or nodes) that validate and record transactions.

Blockchain Technology:

- Cryptocurrency transactions are stored in a digital ledger known as the blockchain. Each block in the chain contains a list of transactions. Once a block is full, it's added to the chain in a linear, chronological order. This system makes it incredibly difficult to alter transaction records, ensuring transparency and trust in the system.

Mining:

- Many cryptocurrencies, including Bitcoin, are created through a process called mining. Mining involves solving complex mathematical problems with computational power to verify transactions and add them to the blockchain. In return for this work, miners are rewarded with new coins.

Wallets:

- To store and manage cryptocurrencies, you need a digital wallet. There are two types of wallets:
  - Hot Wallets: These are online wallets that are connected to the internet, making them easy to use but more vulnerable to hacks.
  - Cold Wallets: These are offline wallets, often in the form of hardware devices, that store cryptocurrency more securely but are less convenient for quick transactions.

Private and Public Keys:

- Cryptocurrencies use public and private keys for security. A public key is similar to an account number, and it's where you receive cryptocurrency. A private key is like a password that gives you access to your funds. Keeping your private key secure is essential because if someone else gains access to it, they can control your cryptocurrency.

Types of Cryptocurrencies

Bitcoin (BTC):

- Bitcoin is the first and most well-known cryptocurrency. It was created in 2009 by an anonymous person or group of people using the pseudonym Satoshi Nakamoto. Bitcoin operates as a store of value and a medium of exchange, though it's often seen more as an investment asset or "digital gold."

Ethereum (ETH):

- Ethereum is a decentralized platform that allows developers to create and deploy smart contracts and decentralized applications (dApps). Ether (ETH) is the cryptocurrency used to pay for transactions and computational services on the Ethereum network. Ethereum is known for its versatility, as it's not just a currency but a platform for decentralized applications.

Ripple (XRP):

- Ripple is both a digital payment network and a cryptocurrency (XRP). Ripple's main goal is to enable fast and low-cost international money transfers, especially for banks and financial institutions. Unlike Bitcoin, Ripple doesn't use mining and instead uses a consensus algorithm to verify transactions.

Litecoin (LTC):

- Litecoin is a peer-to-peer cryptocurrency that was created by Charlie Lee in 2011 as a "lighter" version of Bitcoin. It is faster and more efficient in terms of transaction processing, which makes it a popular choice for smaller, everyday transactions.

Stablecoins:

- Stablecoins are a category of cryptocurrencies designed to have a stable value by being pegged to an underlying asset, like a currency (e.g., the US dollar) or a commodity (e.g., gold). Examples include Tether (USDT) and USD Coin (USDC). Stablecoins aim to combine the benefits of cryptocurrency (such as decentralization) with the stability of traditional assets.

Altcoins:

- Any cryptocurrency other than Bitcoin is referred to as an "altcoin" (alternative coin). Some well-known altcoins include Cardano (ADA), Polkadot (DOT), Solana (SOL), and Binance Coin (BNB). Many altcoins are created to improve upon Bitcoin's limitations or to provide different use cases in the blockchain space.

Benefits of Cryptocurrency

Decentralization:

- Cryptocurrencies are not controlled by a central authority like a bank or government, which can make transactions more transparent and less susceptible to manipulation or interference.

Security:

- Blockchain technology provides high levels of security. Cryptocurrencies use encryption to secure transactions, and once a transaction is recorded on the blockchain, it's immutable, meaning it cannot be altered or erased.

Lower Transaction Costs:

- Traditional financial systems often charge fees for transfers, especially cross-border ones. Cryptocurrency transactions can reduce these costs, especially for international transfers, because they don't require intermediaries such as banks.

Accessibility:

- Cryptocurrencies are accessible to anyone with an internet connection, making it possible for individuals in underbanked or unbanked regions to participate in the global economy.

Potential for High Returns:

- Many early adopters of cryptocurrencies, particularly Bitcoin, have seen significant returns on their investments. Cryptocurrencies are known for their price volatility, which presents opportunities for investors to make substantial profits.

Transparency:

- All cryptocurrency transactions are recorded on the blockchain and are publicly visible. This transparency ensures that transactions are auditable and that bad actors can be identified.

Risks of Cryptocurrency

Volatility:

- Cryptocurrencies are highly volatile and can experience rapid price fluctuations. While this can result in large profits, it can also lead to significant losses, especially for short-term traders.

Regulatory Uncertainty:

- Governments around the world are still figuring out how to regulate cryptocurrencies. In some countries, cryptocurrencies are banned, while others are more accepting. Regulatory changes can create uncertainty, affecting the value and accessibility of cryptocurrencies.

Security Risks:

- While the blockchain is secure, cryptocurrency exchanges, wallets, and other platforms are vulnerable to hacking. If you lose access to your private keys or your exchange is hacked, you could lose all of your funds.

Scams and Fraud:

- The cryptocurrency market is still relatively new, and there have been numerous scams, including Ponzi schemes, phishing attacks, and fraudulent Initial Coin Offerings (ICOs). It's essential to be cautious and do thorough research before investing in any cryptocurrency project.

Limited Acceptance:

- While cryptocurrency adoption is growing, it's still not widely accepted for everyday transactions. Most businesses still prefer traditional forms of payment, meaning cryptocurrencies might not be as useful for day-to-day purchases.

Environmental Impact:

- Some cryptocurrencies, particularly Bitcoin, require large amounts of energy to mine, which can contribute to environmental concerns. Critics argue that the environmental cost of mining cryptocurrencies is unsustainable.

Should You Invest in Cryptocurrency?

Cryptocurrency offers significant potential for growth and can be a powerful tool for diversifying your investment portfolio. However, it also carries risks that require careful consideration. Before investing in cryptocurrency, you should assess:

Risk Tolerance: Are you comfortable with the potential for significant price fluctuations and losses?

Investment Horizon: Are you looking to invest for the long term, or are you hoping to make a quick profit from short-term price movements?

Research: Have you done thorough research into the cryptocurrency you're interested in? Understanding the project, its use case and its underlying technology is crucial.

If you're new to the space, it may be helpful to start small, invest in more established cryptocurrencies like Bitcoin or Ethereum, and consider speaking with a financial advisor. Cryptocurrency can be a valuable addition to your portfolio if you approach it with caution and proper knowledge.

What is an IUL Investment Account?

An Indexed Universal Life (IUL) insurance policy is a type of permanent life insurance that combines a death benefit with a cash value component that is tied to the performance of a stock market index (like the S&P 500). The cash value grows based on the performance of the index, but it is not directly invested in the market. Instead, the insurance company credits interest to your account based on the index's performance, subject to certain caps and floors.

- Cap: The maximum return your cash value can earn based on the index's performance in a given period.
- Floor: The minimum return, which is usually 0%. This means that even if the index performs poorly or loses value, your account won't lose money.
- Flexibility: You can adjust the death benefit and premiums, which adds flexibility to the policy.

How Does an IUL Differ from a Roth IRA?

A Roth IRA (Individual Retirement Account) is a retirement savings account that allows for tax-free growth and tax-free withdrawals in retirement, provided you meet certain conditions. You contribute after-tax dollars to a Roth IRA, and the investments inside the account grow tax-deferred. When you withdraw funds in retirement, they are not taxed.
Here are some key differences:

Purpose:

- IUL: Primarily a life insurance product with a savings/investment component. It provides a death benefit along with the potential for cash value growth.
- Roth IRA: A retirement savings account designed to provide tax-free growth and withdrawals for retirement. The goal is to grow your investments and provide income in retirement.

Risk & Return:

- IUL: The return is based on the performance of a stock market index but is typically capped at a certain percentage. It has a floor (usually 0%), meaning you won't lose money in a poor market year, but the growth potential is limited by the cap.
- Roth IRA: The return depends on the investments you choose (stocks, bonds, ETFs, etc.). There is no cap on returns, but the downside is that you could lose money if your investments perform poorly.

Investment Options:

- IUL: The cash value grows based on an index's performance, but you don't have direct control over specific investments. The interest is credited based on the index's performance.
- Roth IRA: You can choose your investments—stocks, bonds, mutual funds, ETFs, etc. The returns depend on the performance of those investments.

Tax Treatment:

- IUL: The cash value grows tax-deferred, and you can borrow against it tax-free, though withdrawals or loans may be subject to interest. However, the death benefit is paid out tax-free to beneficiaries.
- Roth IRA: Your investments grow tax-deferred, and qualified withdrawals are tax-free (after the age of 59½ and if the account has been open for at least 5 years).

1. Contribution Limits:
    - IUL: There are no specific annual contribution limits, but there are premium limits based on your age, health, and policy type.
    - Roth IRA: There are annual contribution limits set by the IRS. For 2025, the contribution limit is $6,500 (or $7,500 if you're 50 or older), and eligibility depends on your income level.

Which Gives a Better Return and Interest Rate?

- IUL:
    - The return is generally lower than what you could achieve by investing directly in the stock market due to the cap on interest.
    - However, the floor (0%) provides some downside protection, meaning you won't lose money in a bad market year.
    - Typical returns in an IUL range from 4% to 8% per year, but this depends on the performance of the chosen index, the cap, and the insurer's terms.
- Roth IRA:
    - The return can be higher, depending on how you invest your contributions. If you invest in stocks, the historical average annual return of the stock market (S&P 500) is around 7% to 10% after inflation over the long term.
    - The Roth IRA has no caps, so your returns could be much higher than an IUL if you pick investments that perform well.

Summary of Key Differences

Feature	IUL	Roth IRA
Main Purpose	Life insurance with investment component	Retirement savings account
Investment Control	Limited (linked to an index)	Full control over investments
Return Potential	Limited by cap, with a floor at 0%	No cap, returns based on investments
Risk	No loss of principal (floor of 0%)	Risk of losing principal depending on investments
Tax Treatment	Tax-deferred growth, tax-free death benefit	Tax-free growth and withdrawals
Contribution Limits	No specific limits	Annual contribution limits ($6,500 or $7,500 for over 50)
Target Audience	Those seeking life insurance and investment combined	Those seeking to save for retirement with tax advantages

Which is Better?

- For Retirement Growth: If your main goal is long-term retirement savings and growth, a Roth IRA is likely to provide better returns over time due to the lack of caps on growth and the ability to choose high-performing investments.
- For Life Insurance & Safe Growth: If you're looking for a combination of life insurance with some investment benefits and a guaranteed minimum return (no loss in bad years), an IUL might be more suitable, but the return potential is often more limited than a Roth IRA.

In general, Roth IRAs tend to have higher long-term returns, but IULs can be appealing for those seeking life insurance with some investment growth potential and downside protection.

Diversification: Don’t Put All Your Eggs in One Basket

Diversification is a strategy that helps reduce risk by spreading your investments across various asset types. For example, if you focus solely on tech stocks and the tech sector experiences a downturn, your entire portfolio could take a hit. However, by diversifying into other sectors, such as healthcare or consumer goods, or adding different asset classes like bonds or real estate, you can minimize the impact of any single investment’s poor performance. This way, even if one area of your portfolio suffers, the others can help balance it out, providing greater stability and lowering overall risk.

The Role of Time in Investing

Time is your greatest ally. The longer your money stays invested, the more it benefits from compound growth. This is why it’s essential to start as early as possible, even with small amounts.

Common Investing Mistakes to Avoid

EMOTIONAL DECISIONS

Reacting to market fluctuations can lead to buying high and selling low. Stick to your plan.

LACK OF RESEARCH

Invest in assets you understand.

IGNORING FEES

High fees can eat into your returns. Look for low-cost investment options.

NOT STARTING EARLY

Waiting to invest means missing out on years of potential growth.

KEY TAKEAWAYS

- Investing is essential for long-term wealth building.
- Start small, define your goals, and choose investments that align with your risk tolerance.
- Diversify your portfolio to minimize risk.
- Time in the market beats timing the market—start as early as you can.

ACTION STEPS TO TAKE NOW:

- Identify your primary investment goal (e.g., retirement, education fund, passive income).
- Open an investment account on a beginner-friendly platform.
- Research one type of investment (e.g., stocks or ETFs) and make a small initial investment.
- Commit to contributing regularly, even if it's a small amount each month.

PERSONAL FINANCE

LEARN TO MASTER YOUR MONEY & IMPROVE YOUR LIFE

CHAPTER 06

FINANCIAL PLANNING FOR LIFE EVENTS

FINANCIAL PLANNING FOR LIFE EVENTS

"Prepare Today for a Stable Tomorrow"

Life is full of milestones, and each one brings its own set of financial challenges. Whether you're buying your first home, saving for your child's education, or planning for retirement, careful and thoughtful planning can transform financial stress into manageable, achievable steps. In this chapter, we'll explore how to plan for these significant life events, helping you build a strong foundation of financial stability and ensuring you're prepared to face them with confidence.

Planning for Major Life Events

Each stage of life brings its own set of financial milestones. Whether it's buying a home, starting a family, or planning for retirement, each major event requires careful planning. For instance, purchasing a home involves saving for a down payment and understanding mortgage terms, while starting a family means budgeting for childcare, medical expenses, and future education. While these events may seem overwhelming, proactive planning can turn them into opportunities for building stability and wealth.

The key is to identify the major events you're likely to face and prioritize them based on your goals. Some events, like retirement, are predictable, while others, like medical emergencies or unexpected job changes, may require a contingency plan. By planning ahead, you can allocate your resources effectively, reduce stress, and ensure you're ready for life's transitions.

How to Financially Prepare for Key Milestones

Financially preparing for key milestones involves planning ahead and taking deliberate steps to ensure you're ready for life's major events. Start by identifying the milestones that are most relevant to your life, such as buying a home, starting a family, or planning for retirement. Once you've identified these goals, create a clear savings and budgeting strategy tailored to each milestone. For example, when buying a home, focus on saving for a down payment and understanding mortgage terms, while for starting a family, account for expenses like childcare, healthcare, and education.

Consider long-term goals, like retirement, by investing in retirement accounts and setting aside funds for the future. Additionally, prepare for unexpected events such as medical emergencies by building an emergency fund and securing adequate insurance. By breaking down each milestone into manageable financial steps, you can allocate resources efficiently, reduce stress, and ensure you're on track to meet each goal with confidence.

Expert Recommendations

Financially preparing for key milestones involves planning ahead and taking deliberate steps to ensure you're ready for life's major events. Start by identifying the milestones that are most relevant to your life, such as buying a home, starting a family, or planning for retirement. Once you've identified these goals, create a clear savings and budgeting strategy tailored to each milestone. For example, when buying a home, focus on saving for a down payment and understanding mortgage terms, while for starting a family, account for expenses like childcare, healthcare, and education. Consider long-term goals, like retirement, by investing in retirement accounts and setting aside funds for the future. Additionally, prepare for unexpected events such as medical emergencies by building an emergency fund and securing adequate insurance. By breaking down each milestone into manageable financial steps, you can allocate resources efficiently, reduce stress, and ensure you're on track to meet each goal with confidence.

Navigating Uncertainty with Confidence

Unforeseen events, like medical emergencies or family crises, can disrupt even the best-laid financial plans. While it's impossible to anticipate every challenge, having a contingency plan can provide reassurance during difficult times. One essential aspect of this plan is insurance—such as health, life, and disability coverage—which helps safeguard you and your loved ones when things go wrong.

In addition to insurance, it's crucial to establish a network of trusted advisors. Financial planners, tax professionals, and legal experts can offer tailored guidance to help you navigate tough decisions. By working with professionals who understand your specific situation, you can make informed choices, protect your wealth, and ensure your financial resources are optimized for any uncertainties life may bring.

Looking Ahead with Optimism

Financial planning for life events goes beyond just managing money t's about building a foundation that supports the life you envision and being prepared to welcome opportunities when they come. By thoughtfully planning for these milestones, you can ease your worries, reduce stress, and feel more confident as you navigate each stage. With a bit of intention and preparation, you can enjoy the journey and embrace whatever comes your way.

Planning for major life events is crucial for one's finances because life is full of changes that often come with big financial costs. By planning, you can ease the financial stress that accompanies milestones and ensure that you're ready to face life's challenges. Whether it's buying a house, starting a family, or preparing for retirement, having a financial plan in place can help you navigate these events with more confidence and security.

Why Is It Important for Finances?
Planning for major life events ensures that you are prepared for the financial implications of these changes. Without preparation, unexpected costs can create stress, lead to debt, or even disrupt your long-term financial goals. When you plan, you're better equipped to manage expenses without sacrificing your financial well-being.

Proper financial planning also helps you prioritize your spending, save for future needs, and invest for long-term goals. It helps you balance short-term desires with long-term needs, ensuring you don't overextend yourself financially.

Types of Life Events Where Savings Are Important:

1. **Buying a Home:** Purchasing a house often requires a significant down payment, closing costs, and ongoing maintenance expenses. Having savings ready can make the process smoother and less stressful.
2. **Starting a Family:** Raising children involves costs such as healthcare, childcare, education, and daily living expenses. Planning for these costs early allows you to provide for your family's needs without financial strain.
3. **Education (for yourself or your children):** Whether you're saving for your college expenses or setting aside money for your child's education, having a savings plan can help avoid relying on student loans or credit cards.
4. **Retirement:** Saving for retirement early helps ensure you'll have enough money to live comfortably when you're no longer working. The earlier you start, the more your savings can grow due to compound interest.
5. **Health Emergencies:** Accidents, illness, or unexpected medical procedures can be costly. Having an emergency fund or health insurance coverage helps protect you from financial hardship during these tough times.
6. **Wedding or Major Life Celebration:** Whether it's a wedding, milestone birthday, or special event, these moments often require significant financial preparation for things like venue costs, catering, or travel.

How to Financially Plan for Milestones:
Set Clear Goals: Identify the major events you anticipate and decide how much money you'll need. Be specific with the amounts and timeline. For example, if you're planning to buy a house in five years, research the average down payment for homes in your area and start saving toward that goal.

Create a Budget: Break down how much money you need to save each month to meet your financial goals. A budget can help you track expenses, reduce unnecessary spending, and allocate more funds toward your savings.

Start an Emergency Fund: An emergency fund is essential for covering unexpected costs, like health issues or car repairs, without derailing your savings for bigger goals. Aim to save at least three to six months' worth of living expenses in an easily accessible account.

1. Utilize Specific Savings Accounts: For major life events, it may be helpful to open separate savings accounts designated for specific purposes—like a house fund, wedding fund, or education fund. This helps you stay organized and focused.
2. Invest for the Long-Term: If the milestone is years away, consider investments that can grow your savings over time, such as stocks, bonds, or retirement accounts. The key is to make your money work for you while keeping in mind the timing of your goals.
3. Review and Adjust Plans Regularly: Life can change, and so can your financial situation. Review your plans and adjust them as necessary—whether it's increasing savings after a raise, changing your spending habits, or shifting your investment strategy based on life changes.

Navigating Uncertainty and Looking Forward with Optimism:
Uncertainty is a natural part of life, and it's impossible to predict everything that might happen. However, by planning for major life events, you create a sense of financial stability that helps you feel more prepared, no matter what challenges arise. Here's how to navigate uncertainty:

1. **Focus on What You Can Control:** While you can't predict every life event, you can control how much you save and how well you manage your finances. Focus on building a solid foundation with savings, insurance, and investments.
2. **Be Flexible:** Life doesn't always go according to plan, and you might face unexpected challenges. Be open to adjusting your goals or timeline when needed, and don't be too hard on yourself if things don't go exactly as planned.
3. **Stay Positive:** A positive mindset can help you stay motivated, even during tough times. Knowing that you've taken steps to prepare financially can give you peace of mind and allow you to approach life's challenges with confidence.
4. **Build a Support System**: Surround yourself with trusted advisors, like financial planners or mentors, who can guide you through tough decisions. Having a strong support system can help you navigate uncertain times with a clearer perspective.

By planning ahead and preparing for life's milestones, you can reduce stress, stay focused on your goals, and move forward with optimism. Whether it's buying a home, saving for education, or securing a comfortable retirement, the key is to take proactive steps now that will pay off in the future.

CHAPTER 07

RETIREMENT PLANNING

fruits of your hard work. Achieving a comfortable retirement requires intentional planning and disciplined action, no matter your age or current financial situation. This chapter will guide you through the essentials of retirement planning, helping you prepare for a future where financial security meets personal fulfillment.

Why Retirement Planning Matters

Retirement planning matters because it helps ensure that you can live comfortably and securely when you no longer have a steady paycheck. By starting early and saving consistently, you give yourself the opportunity to accumulate enough wealth to support your lifestyle in retirement, whether that means traveling, pursuing hobbies, or simply enjoying peace of mind without financial stress.

Without proper planning, you may face unexpected challenges as you age, such as rising healthcare costs or outliving your savings. Retirement planning also allows you to take advantage of tax benefits and investment growth, helping your money work for you over time. Ultimately, it's about creating the financial freedom to enjoy your later years without worrying about your financial security.

Calculating How Much You'll Need

Calculating how much you'll need for retirement involves considering several key factors to estimate your future expenses and ensure you can maintain your desired lifestyle once you stop working. Start by thinking about your anticipated monthly expenses, including housing, food, healthcare, transportation, and leisure activities.

Keep in mind that some expenses may decrease in retirement (like work-related costs), while others may rise (such as healthcare). A general rule of thumb is that you may need around 70-80% of your pre-retirement income annually to maintain your lifestyle.

Building Your Retirement Fund

There are several ways to save for retirement, and the best strategy often combines multiple approaches:

- **Employer-Sponsored Plans:** Contributing to a 401(k) or similar plan allows you to save pre-tax dollars, often with an employer match. Maximize this benefit whenever possible.
- **Individual Retirement Accounts (IRAs):** IRAs provide tax advantages for retirement savings. Traditional IRAs offer tax-deferred growth, while Roth IRAs allow tax-free withdrawals in retirement.
- **Brokerage Accounts:** For those who've maxed out tax-advantaged accounts, investing in a regular brokerage account can supplement your retirement savings.
- **Pensions:** If you're eligible for a pension plan, include it in your retirement income projections, and understand how benefits are calculated.

Investing for Retirement

Long-term growth is essential to building your retirement fund, and investing plays a significant role. Diversify your portfolio to balance risk and reward, allocating assets among stocks, bonds, and other investments based on your risk tolerance and time horizon.

- **In Your 20s and 30s:** Focus on growth-oriented investments like stocks. Time is on your side, allowing you to ride out market fluctuations.
- **In Your 40s and 50s:** Gradually shift to a more balanced portfolio that includes bonds and other low-risk assets to preserve gains.
- **In Your 60s and Beyond:** Prioritize stability and income-generating investments to ensure consistent cash flow during retirement.

Social Security and Other Income Sources

Social Security benefits can supplement your retirement savings, but they're rarely enough to cover all expenses. Check your eligibility and estimated benefits through the Social Security Administration website. Other potential income sources include rental properties, part-time work, or annuities, all of which can diversify and stabilize your retirement income.

Why Retirement Planning Matters

Building your retirement fund requires a strategic and consistent approach. The earlier you start saving, the more time your money has to grow through compound interest. Here are some key steps to help you build your retirement fund:

Start Early: The earlier you begin saving, the more time your investments have to grow. Even small contributions made early on can have a significant impact over time due to the power of compound interest.

Contribute Regularly: Set up automatic contributions to your retirement accounts, such as a 401(k), IRA, or other retirement plans. This ensures you're consistently saving and helps you stay disciplined in your savings habits.

Take Advantage of Employer Matching: If your employer offers a matching contribution to your 401(k), make sure you contribute enough to take full advantage of the match. This is essentially "free" money that can help grow your retirement savings faster.

Choose the Right Retirement Accounts: Different retirement accounts offer different benefits. A 401(k) allows you to contribute pre-tax money and often includes employer matching. An IRA (Individual Retirement Account) gives you more control over your investments and offers tax advantages. Consider speaking to a financial advisor to determine which options are best for you based on your financial goals.

Invest Wisely: Diversify your investments to reduce risk and maximize returns. This might include a mix of stocks, bonds, and other investment vehicles. As you get closer to retirement, you may want to shift to more conservative investments to protect your savings from market volatility.

Increase Contributions Over Time: As your income grows, aim to increase the amount you're contributing to your retirement accounts. You can also increase contributions whenever you receive a raise or bonus.

Monitor and Adjust: Regularly review your retirement plan and investments to make sure you're on track. Life circumstances and market conditions can change, so be prepared to adjust your savings strategy if necessary.

Avoid Early Withdrawals: Taking money out of your retirement accounts before retirement can severely impact your long-term savings due to penalties and lost growth potential. It's important to treat these funds as long-term savings to secure your future.

Investing for Retirement

Investing for retirement is a crucial part of building long-term financial security. The goal is to create a retirement portfolio that grows over time, allowing you to retire comfortably without worrying about running out of money. Here's how to approach investing for retirement:

Choose the Right Accounts

To maximize your retirement savings, take advantage of tax-advantaged accounts like 401(k)s, IRAs (Individual Retirement Accounts), or Roth IRAs. These accounts allow your money to grow tax-deferred (traditional 401(k) and IRA) or tax-free (Roth IRA), depending on the account type.

- 401(k): Offered by many employers, it allows for automatic contributions from your paycheck, often with the benefit of employer matching contributions.
- IRA: You can open this account independently. A traditional IRA offers tax-deductible contributions, while a Roth IRA allows for tax-free withdrawals in retirement, provided certain conditions are met.

Diversify Your Investments

Building a diversified portfolio helps manage risk and increases your chances of earning steady returns over time. A good retirement portfolio usually includes a mix of:

- Stocks: These are riskier but have the potential for higher returns. They're suitable for younger investors with a long time horizon.
- Bonds: These are lower risk and provide more stable, predictable returns, making them ideal as you get closer to retirement.
- Mutual Funds and ETFs: These funds allow you to invest in a broad array of assets, such as stocks and bonds, making diversification easier and more affordable.
- Real Estate and Other Assets: Including other investment types, like real estate or commodities, can add another layer of diversification to your portfolio.

Start Early and Contribute Consistently

The earlier you start investing for retirement, the more time your money has to grow. Consistent contributions, even if small, can build up significantly over time thanks to compound interest. Automating your contributions to your retirement account helps ensure that you stay on track and invest regularly.

Take Advantage of Employer Matching

If your employer offers a 401(k) match, make sure you contribute enough to take full advantage of it. This is essentially free money that can significantly boost your retirement savings.

Understand Your Risk Tolerance

Your age, financial goals, and personal risk tolerance will influence your investment strategy. When you're young, you can afford to take more risks by investing in stocks or stock-heavy mutual funds. As you approach retirement, you may want to shift to more stable, income-generating investments like bonds to reduce risk.

Rebalance Your Portfolio

As your investments grow, certain assets may take up a larger portion of your portfolio than you originally intended. Regularly rebalancing—adjusting your investments to maintain your desired asset allocation—helps ensure your portfolio stays aligned with your goals and risk tolerance.

Stay Focused on the Long-Term

Investing for retirement is a long-term strategy. Avoid reacting to short-term market fluctuations or trying to time the market, as this can lead to emotional decision-making and missed opportunities. Stay focused on your long-term goals and let your investments grow over time.

Consider Professional Guidance

If you're unsure where to start or need help managing your retirement investments, a financial advisor can help you develop a strategy that's tailored to your goals. They can provide insight into asset allocation, tax-efficient strategies, and ensure that your portfolio is set up for long-term growth.

By choosing the right retirement accounts, diversifying your investments, and contributing regularly, you can build a retirement fund that will support you when you're ready to retire. It's never too early to start planning for your future, and every step you take today brings you closer to a financially secure tomorrow.

Planning for Healthcare Costs

Healthcare often becomes a significant expense in retirement. Consider opening a Health Savings Account (HSA) during your working years to save tax-advantaged funds for medical expenses. Additionally, research Medicare options and supplemental insurance plans to ensure you're adequately covered.

Staying Flexible and Reviewing Your Plan

Life is unpredictable, and your retirement plan should adapt to changing circumstances. Regularly review your savings, investments, and projected expenses to ensure you're on track. Major life changes, like marriage, divorce, or career shifts, may require adjustments to your strategy.

KEY TAKEAWAYS

- Start saving for retirement as early as possible to benefit from compound growth.
- Estimate your retirement needs and account for inflation.
- Diversify your savings and investment strategies to balance growth and stability.
- Consider all potential income sources, including Social Security, pensions, and passive income.

ACTION STEPS TO TAKE NOW:

- Calculate your retirement savings target using an online calculator.
- Maximize contributions to employer-sponsored plans and IRAs.
- Diversify your investments based on your time horizon and risk tolerance.
- Set a reminder to review your retirement plan annually and adjust as needed.

CHAPTER 08

FINANCIAL LITERACY & YOUTH

C H A P T E R 0 8

FINANCIAL LITERACY & YOUTH

“Set the Next Generation up for Financial Success”

In a world where money affects so many parts of our lives, teaching kids how to manage it is one of the best gifts you can give them. Learning about money helps young learners make smart choices, develop good habits, and prepare for a secure future. This chapter will show you fun and easy ways to teach these important lessons to young learnersof different ages.

Why Educate on Financial Literacy Early?

Educating kids about financial literacy early is important because it gives them the skills they need to make smart money choices throughout their lives. When kids learn about money early on, they develop good habits like saving, budgeting, and understanding the value of money. These lessons can help them avoid common mistakes later, like overspending or getting into debt. Teaching financial literacy early also helps kids feel more confident and in control when it comes to managing their money, which is an essential skill for a successful future. By starting young, we give them the tools they need to make informed decisions and build a strong financial foundation.

Understand the value of money and work.

Differentiate between wants and needs.

Build a foundation for saving, budgeting, and investing.

Instilling these skills ensures that your children grow into adults who can manage their finances confidently and responsibly.

Start with the Basics

For younger kids, it’s important to keep lessons about money simple and easy to understand. Start by talking about the different types of money, like coins, paper bills, and digital payments. Explain where money comes from and how people use it to buy things. You can use real-life situations, like going grocery shopping, to show how budgeting works. For example, give them a small amount of money to spend and let them decide what to buy within that limit.

As kids get older, you can introduce more advanced ideas, like why it’s important to save money for the future or explain the difference between credit cards and debit cards.

Engaging Activities to Teach Financial Skills

ALLOWANCE AS A TEACHING TOOL

Give children a small, consistent allowance and encourage them to allocate it for different purposes, like spending, saving, and giving. This provides hands-on experience in money management.

ROLE-PLAYING GAMES

Simulate real-life scenarios like running a shop or budgeting for a birthday party. This makes learning interactive and fun.

SAVINGS GOALS

Help children set a specific savings goal, such as buying a toy or contributing to a family outing. Use a clear jar or a savings app so they can visually track their progress.

CHORES FOR EXTRA CASH

Teach the value of work by assigning paid chores. Link earnings to effort and responsibility, helping children understand how money is earned.

Introduce Advanced Concepts to Teens

For teenagers, expand financial literacy to include topics like:

- **Budgeting:** Show them how to create a simple budget to track income, expenses, and savings.
- **Banking Basics:** Teach them how to open and manage a bank account, understand statements, and avoid overdrafts.
- **Earning Money:** Encourage part-time jobs or entrepreneurial ventures like tutoring or selling handmade goods.
- **Credit and Loans:** Explain how credit works, the importance of a credit score, and the risks of debt.
- **Investing:** Introduce the concept of stocks, bonds, and compound interest to spark curiosity about long-term financial growth.

Allowance as a Teaching Tool

Allowance is a great teaching tool for kids because it gives them hands-on experience with managing money. By having their own money to spend, save, or even share, kids learn important lessons about budgeting and making choices. It helps them understand the value of money and the consequences of spending it too quickly. For example, if they spend all their allowance in one week, they'll learn they may not have enough for something they want later. Allowance also encourages saving for bigger goals, like buying a special toy or saving for the future. It's a fun, practical way to teach kids about responsibility, decision-making, and the importance of money management in everyday life.

An allowance teaches children valuable lessons about money management, responsibility, and decision-making. It helps kids learn how to budget, save, spend wisely, and understand the value of earning money. By handling their own allowance, children get a chance to practice these skills in a safe environment, making mistakes and learning from them before they have to manage larger amounts of money as adults.

As a parent, the long-term goals of establishing an allowance are to help your child develop healthy financial habits and a strong understanding of how money works. It's about teaching them to plan ahead, set goals, and make informed choices about spending and saving. An allowance can also encourage a sense of independence and confidence as they learn how to manage their own resources.

As the child grows, these lessons will benefit them in adulthood, especially when it comes to Activities of Daily Living (ADL) skills. ADLs include things like managing personal finances, budgeting for daily expenses, and saving for future goals—skills that are essential for independent living. By learning these skills through allowance, children will be better prepared to handle their finances responsibly as adults. They will understand how to prioritize their needs, plan for their future, and make informed choices that lead to financial stability and independence.

Role-Playing Games

Simulations are important because they provide a hands-on, interactive way to learn real-life skills in a safe and controlled environment. Instead of just talking about concepts like budgeting, saving, or managing money, simulations allow individuals—especially kids and young learners—to experience these situations firsthand. Here's why they're so valuable:

1. **Active Learning:** Simulations engage participants actively, making learning more memorable and effective. By doing things like running a shop or planning a budget, learners can see the outcomes of their choices in real-time, helping them grasp concepts better.
2. **Building Confidence:** When kids practice financial decision-making through simulations, they build confidence in their ability to manage money and solve problems. They can make mistakes, learn from them, and try again without the real-world consequences.
3. **Real-Life Skill Development:** Simulations teach practical, real-world skills such as budgeting, time management, critical thinking, and decision-making. These skills will help kids when they are older and need to manage their personal finances or make important life decisions.
4. **Safe to Make Mistakes:** Unlike actual financial situations, simulations allow learners to make mistakes in a risk-free way. For example, if a child overspends in a simulation, they can immediately see how that affects their budget and learn from it, without real-world consequences like running out of money.
5. **Engagement and Motivation:** Simulations are fun! They turn learning into a game-like experience, which keeps kids engaged and motivated. When learning feels fun, children are more likely to retain what they've learned and apply it in the future.
6. **Building Problem-Solving Skills:** In simulations, learners often face challenges (like running out of money or needing to make a tough decision). These situations encourage problem-solving, critical thinking, and creativity, all of which are valuable life skills.

Overall, simulations make learning more dynamic and practical, helping learners feel prepared for real-life situations and giving them the tools to make smarter decisions.

Savings Goals

What Are Savings Goals for Youth?

Savings goals for youth can vary depending on their age, interests, and life stage. Here are some examples of savings goals for young people:

1. **Short-Term Goals:**
    - Saving for a special toy, game, or hobby.
    - Setting aside money for a concert, event, or sports ticket.
    - Saving for a weekend trip with friends or family.
2. **Mid-Term Goals:**
    - Saving for a bike, phone, or other big-ticket item.
    - Setting aside money for summer camp, a school trip, or other educational experiences.
    - Saving for their first car or a part of the down payment.
3. **Long-Term Goals:**
    - Saving for college tuition or a study abroad program.
    - Saving for their first apartment or starting a business.
    - Contributing to a retirement fund (like a Roth IRA or other investment account) to start early.

Why Are Savings Goals Important for Youth?

Savings goals are important for youth because they teach young people the value of money and help them develop essential life skills that will serve them well into adulthood. Here are some reasons why savings goals are so important:

- **Building Financial Discipline:** Setting savings goals helps youth understand the importance of budgeting and planning. It encourages them to make thoughtful decisions about how to spend and save their money.

- **Learning Delayed Gratification:** Having savings goals teaches young people the power of patience. It shows them how to plan for something they want, rather than spending impulsively. This ability to delay gratification is a key life skill that will help them succeed in various areas of their lives.

- **Encouraging Responsibility:** When youth set and work toward savings goals, they learn responsibility. They take ownership of their money, decisions, and future financial well-being.

- **Understanding the Value of Money:** By saving for specific goals, youth gain a better understanding of how money works and the effort required to achieve financial goals. It also helps them understand the importance of earning and saving for future needs.

- **Starting Financial Independence:** The earlier youth start saving and setting goals, the sooner they can start to build financial independence. They begin to recognize that they are in control of their financial future and can make decisions that will lead to long-term financial success.

What Benefits Are Offered to Youth Who Understand the Power of Savings and Have Goals for Their Adulthood?

Youth who understand the power of savings and set goals for their future will experience several long-term benefits in adulthood. Some of the key benefits include:

- **Financial Security:** When youth develop the habit of saving early, they are more likely to have a solid financial foundation in adulthood. This habit will help them manage expenses, handle emergencies, and avoid debt.

- **Less Financial Stress:** Those who practice saving and setting goals will experience less financial stress in the future. Having an emergency fund or saving for major expenses, like a home or education, can provide peace of mind and prevent anxiety about money.

- **Better Money Management:** Youth who set and work toward savings goals learn important financial skills, such as budgeting, tracking expenses, and prioritizing needs over wants. These skills will help them make smart decisions about how to handle money as adults.

- **Early Start on Wealth Building:** By learning to save and invest early, youth can take advantage of the power of compound interest. This allows their money to grow over time, helping them build wealth for the future. For example, saving a little money for retirement in their teens can lead to a large sum by the time they retire.

- **Achieving Major Life Goals:** Whether it's buying a home, traveling the world, starting a business, or funding their child's education, youth who start saving early are more likely to achieve their long-term life goals. By setting financial goals and working toward them, they create the opportunity to live the life they want.

- **Increased Confidence:** Learning how to manage money and set goals boosts a young person's confidence. They will feel empowered knowing they have the skills to plan for the future, make good decisions, and achieve their dreams.

- **Improved Financial Independence:** Youth who understand the value of saving and goal-setting will be better equipped to live independently when they're older. They'll have the financial tools and knowledge to manage their finances, avoid excessive debt, and support themselves without relying on others.

- **Better Career Choices:** Understanding money early on also helps youth make smarter career choices. They may prioritize jobs with good benefits, savings plans, or opportunities for growth, leading to a more financially secure and fulfilling career path.

Savings goals are a powerful tool for youth, helping them build financial literacy, responsibility, and discipline. Understanding how to save and having clear goals for the future empowers young people to take charge of their finances and prepare for a successful adulthood. By learning the importance of saving early on, they can create a foundation for financial security, independence, and peace of mind throughout their lives.

Financial Tools for Kids and Teens

Leverage age-appropriate tools to reinforce lessons:

APPS FOR KIDS

Apps like Greenlight or RoosterMoney help kids learn budgeting and saving in a fun, interactive way.

BOOKS

Choose engaging books about money management designed for young readers.

VISUAL CHARTS

Use goal-setting charts or allowance trackers to keep kids motivated.

Modeling Good Financial Habits

Children learn as much from observation as from instruction. Be mindful of how you discuss and handle money in front of them. Demonstrate budgeting, saving, and thoughtful spending. Involve them in family financial decisions, like planning a vacation or grocery shopping, to show how these habits play out in real life.

Encouraging Financial Independence

The ultimate goal is to prepare children for financial independence. Start small by giving them autonomy over their allowance and gradually involve them in larger decisions as they mature. Encourage them to make mistakes and learn from them in a safe environment.

KEY TAKEAWAYS

- Introduce financial concepts early and adapt lessons as young learners grow.
- Use real-life scenarios and interactive activities to make learning engaging.
- Gradually introduce advanced topics like budgeting, credit, and investing.
- Model positive financial habits and involve children in family financial decisions.

ACTION STEPS TO TAKE NOW:

- Set up an allowance system that includes spending, saving, and giving categories.
- Identify a savings goal with your child and help them create a plan to achieve it.
- Research and download a kid-friendly financial app to make learning interactive.
- Schedule a family activity where financial decisions are part of the process, like budgeting for a day out.

PERSONAL FINANCE

LEARN TO MASTER YOUR MONEY & IMPROVE YOUR LIFE

CHAPTER 09

BUILD A WEALTH MINDSET

CHAPTER 09

BUILD A WEALTH MINDSET

"Shift Your Mind, Secure Your Finances"

Financial success isn't just about numbers—it's also about mindset. Your beliefs, attitudes, and habits play a significant role in how you handle money and build wealth. Developing a wealth mindset empowers you to approach finances with confidence, resilience, and a focus on long-term growth. This chapter explores how to cultivate that mindset and break free from limiting beliefs about money.

Understanding a Wealth Mindset

A wealth mindset is an outlook that prioritizes abundance, growth, and strategic decision-making. It contrasts with a scarcity mindset, which focuses on fear, lack, and limitations. People with a wealth mindset see opportunities where others see obstacles, making proactive choices that align with their financial goals.

The Power of Beliefs About Money

Your relationship with money often stems from childhood experiences and cultural influences. Reflect on what you learned about money growing up. Were you taught that money is scarce and must be hoarded? Or did you learn that it's a tool for creating opportunities? Understanding these beliefs is the first step toward shifting them.

For instance, if you believe, "I'll never earn enough to save," challenge that thought. Replace it with, "I can start small and build my savings over time." Positive, actionable beliefs help reframe your perspective and open the door to financial possibilities.

Key Habits for Building a Wealth Mindset

FOCUS ON GROWTH, NOT JUST SAVINGS

While saving is essential, focus on growing your income through skill development, investments, or side hustles. Wealth isn't just about cutting expenses; it's about expanding opportunities.

EMBRACE LIFELONG LEARNING

Stay curious about finances. Read books, attend workshops, and seek advice from experts. A commitment to learning equips you with the knowledge needed to make informed choices.

PRACTICE GRATITUDE

Acknowledge what you already have. Gratitude shifts your mindset from scarcity to abundance, encouraging you to make thoughtful, intentional financial decisions.

SET BIG, BOLD GOALS

Think beyond paying bills or building an emergency fund. Dream big—whether it's starting your own business, retiring early, or creating a legacy for future generations.

CELEBRATE SMALL WINS

Progress, no matter how small, is worth celebrating. Whether it's saving your first $100 or sticking to your budget for a month, acknowledging milestones reinforces positive habits.

Overcoming Money Anxiety

Many people struggle with money anxiety, often rooted in fear of making mistakes or scarcity. To overcome this, focus on the aspects of your finances you can control. Break larger goals into smaller, manageable steps, and remind yourself that progress takes time. Seeking guidance from a financial coach or therapist can also help address deep-seated fears about money.

Visualizing Success

Visualization is a powerful tool for building a wealth mindset. Take a moment each day to picture your ideal financial future. Imagine the freedom, security, and opportunities you'll create. This practice keeps you motivated and focused on your goals.

Create a vision board to make these dreams tangible. Include images, words, and symbols that represent your financial aspirations, whether it's a dream home, a travel destination, or a thriving business.

Overcoming Money Anxiety

Overcoming money anxiety is an important step toward gaining control of your financial well-being and building a healthier relationship with money. Money anxiety can stem from many sources: fear of not having enough, worry about making the wrong financial decisions or feeling overwhelmed by debt. Whatever the cause, it's important to understand that financial challenges are common, and with the right tools and mindset, they can be addressed.

Here's how to overcome money anxiety:

Understand the Root Cause

Start by understanding what specifically triggers your money anxiety. Is it mounting debt? The pressure of saving for the future? Living paycheck to paycheck? By identifying the source, you can address it directly. This self-awareness is the first step toward managing your anxiety.

Create a Clear Financial Plan

A well-thought-out financial plan can provide a sense of control and direction. Break down your financial situation into manageable steps. Create a budget that outlines your income, expenses, and savings goals. By having a clear picture of your financial health, you can reduce the fear of the unknown.

- Track Your Spending: Keeping track of where your money goes each month can help you identify areas where you can cut back and start saving.
- Set Specific Goals: Having clear short-term and long-term financial goals, such as saving for an emergency fund or paying off debt, can provide motivation and focus.

Focus on What You Can Control

Money anxiety often comes from worrying about things that are out of your control, such as the cost of living or unexpected financial events. Instead of dwelling on what you can't change, focus on what you can control. This includes creating and sticking to a budget, avoiding unnecessary expenses, and building good financial habits.

Build an Emergency Fund

Having a financial cushion can reduce anxiety because it offers security in case of unexpected expenses, like a medical emergency or car repair. Start small, even if it's just setting aside a few dollars a week. Knowing that you have a safety net can give you peace of mind and reduce the fear of financial uncertainty.

Take Small, Consistent Actions

Overcoming money anxiety isn't about making huge changes overnight. Start with small, manageable steps that you can consistently follow. Whether it's automating savings or setting aside a small amount of money for debt repayment, taking action—no matter how small—helps build confidence and momentum.

Educate Yourself

Knowledge is a powerful tool for reducing financial stress. The more you understand about budgeting, debt management, investing, and saving, the less overwhelming money can feel. Educate yourself through books, podcasts, or financial workshops. The more informed you are, the more confident you'll feel in your financial decisions.

Practice Mindfulness

Money anxiety can often be worsened by negative thoughts and stress about the future. Practicing mindfulness or relaxation techniques, such as meditation, deep breathing, or journaling, can help you manage stress. Mindfulness helps you stay present and avoid spiraling into worry about hypothetical financial situations.

Seek Support

It's okay to ask for help. Talking about money, even if it feels uncomfortable, can make a big difference. You might find comfort in discussing your financial worries with a trusted friend or family member. If needed, seeking professional guidance from a financial planner or counselor can offer a fresh perspective and provide strategies for overcoming financial anxiety.

Challenge Negative Beliefs About Money

Sometimes, money anxiety comes from deeply ingrained beliefs about money, such as "I'll never be able to get ahead" or "I'm bad with money." Challenge these beliefs by reminding yourself of past successes, even small ones. Reframe your mindset by focusing on progress and the positive steps you're taking, rather than on perceived failures.

Take Care of Your Mental Health

Financial anxiety can often be linked to stress or underlying mental health issues. If your anxiety feels overwhelming or persistent, consider seeking professional help from a therapist or counselor. They can help you address the emotional side of money anxiety and provide coping mechanisms for dealing with stress.

Celebrate Small Wins

As you make progress toward your financial goals, take time to celebrate small victories. Whether it's paying off a credit card, reaching a savings goal, or sticking to your budget for a month, acknowledging these wins can build confidence and help you stay motivated.

Overcoming money anxiety isn't about getting rid of every financial worry it's about taking steps to manage and reduce stress around money. By creating a financial plan, focusing on what you can control, educating yourself, and seeking support when needed, you can build a healthier, more positive relationship with your finances. Small, consistent actions add up over time, helping you feel more in control and empowered to handle financial challenges with confidence.

The Role of Generosity in Wealth Building

True wealth isn't just about accumulating money—it's also about giving back. Generosity fosters connection, gratitude, and purpose. Whether it's donating to a cause you care about or mentoring someone in need, giving reinforces the idea that wealth is about creating positive change, not just personal gain.

Reframing Setbacks

Financial setbacks are inevitable, but they don't have to derail your progress. Instead of seeing setbacks as failures, view them as learning opportunities. Ask yourself: What can I do differently next time? How can I use this experience to grow? Resilience is a cornerstone of a wealth mindset.

KEY TAKEAWAYS

- A wealth mindset prioritizes growth, abundance, and strategic decision-making.
- Challenge limiting beliefs and replace them with empowering ones.
- Embrace habits like gratitude, lifelong learning, and goal-setting to foster a positive financial outlook.
- Use visualization and generosity to align your finances with your values and aspirations.

ACTION STEPS TO TAKE NOW:

- Write down one limiting belief about money and reframe it into a positive, actionable statement.
- Create a vision board that represents your financial goals and display it where you'll see it daily.
- Identify one skill you want to learn to increase your income potential and research resources to develop it.
- Commit to celebrating one small financial win this week to reinforce positive habits.

CHAPTER 10

FORWARD-LOOKING FINANCIAL JOURNEY

FORWARD-LOOKING: FINANCIAL JOURNEY

"Small Steps Now, Big Achievements Later"

Congratulations on taking the first step toward investing in your financial knowledge and future! It's a big achievement, and every chapter of this toolkit has been designed to provide you with the tools, insights, and practical strategies to help you build a life filled with financial confidence and independence. Whether you're just starting or refining a plan that's already in motion, remember that financial growth is a journey, and it unfolds one step at a time. Be patient with yourself, embrace each milestone, and know that every decision, no matter how small, is a positive move toward securing your future. You've got this!

The Importance of Consistency

Consistency is key to achieving long-term success. Small, steady actions compound over time, helping you build habits, reach goals, and overcome challenges. Whether it's saving money, building skills, or maintaining healthy routines, consistency creates lasting progress and confidence in your abilities.

Your Financial Journey is Personal

Your financial journey is personal, unique to your goals, values, and circumstances. There's no one-size-fits-all approach, and what works for someone else may not be the best for you. It's about making decisions that align with your vision for the future, staying true to your priorities, and understanding that your path may evolve over time. Embrace your journey with patience and confidence, knowing that it's yours to shape.

A Final Word of Encouragement & Resources

You're doing something truly powerful by taking the time to learn about financial management. The knowledge you're gaining now will not only set you up for a more secure future but will also have a lasting, positive impact on your family's well-being. By managing money wisely, you're building a foundation that can provide stability, opportunities, and peace of mind for those you love. Remember, every step you take, no matter how small, is progress. Stay patient with yourself, keep learning, and know that the effort you put into managing your finances today will create a brighter, more sustainable tomorrow for you and your family. You've got this!

KEY TAKEAWAYS

- Consistency and persistence are the cornerstones of financial success.
- Your financial journey is personal—define what wealth and stability mean to you.
- Embrace setbacks as learning opportunities and focus on long-term growth.
- Celebrate progress, no matter how small, and stay committed to your goals.

Monthly Budget
PLANNER

MONTH:

INCOME

DATE	DESCRIPTION	AMOUNT	PAID
			☐
			☐
			☐
			☐
			☐

EXPENSES

DATE	EXPENSES	AMOUNT	PAID
			☐
			☐
			☐
			☐
			☐
			☐
			☐
			☐
			☐
			☐
	TOTAL		

MONTHLY

	GOAL	ACTUAL	DIFFERENCE
INCOME			
BUDGET			
SAVINGS			
EXPENSES			

DAILY SPENDING

TOTAL:

BUDGET *planner*

INCOME	AMOUNT
TOTAL:	

DEBT	PAID
TOTAL:	

FIXED EXPENSES	BUDGET	SPENT
	TOTAL:	

VARIABLE EXPENSES	BUDGET	SPENT
	TOTAL:	

SAVINGS	SAVED
TOTAL:	

TOTAL BUDGET		-	TOTAL SPENT		=	

Vacation Budget Planner (sample)

Duration : 5 Days

Destination : Florida- Key West

No.	Category	Details	Estimated Cost (USD)	Subtotal (USD)
1	Transportation	Flight Tickets (Round Trip)	$200	$280
		Local Transport (Car/Bike Rental)	$60	
		Fuel/Parking	$20	
2	Accommodation	Hotel/Villa (4 Nights)	$250	$250
3	Food & Drinks	Meals (5 Days, approx. $10/day)	$50	$70
		Snacks/Drinks	$20	
4	Activities & Fun	Entrance Fees (Tourist Spots)	$35	$140
		Water Sports/Adventure Activities	$70	
		Souvenirs/Shopping	$35	
5	Miscellaneous	Emergency Fund	$35	$35
	Total			$775

Note :

Vacation Budget Planner

Duration :

Destination :

No.	Category	Details	Estimated Cost (USD)	Subtotal (USD)
	Total			

Note :

SAVINGS Tracker...

YEAR OF	SAVING FOR	AMOUNT NEEDED

MONTH	WEEK 1	WEEK 2	WEEK 3	WEEK 4	TOTAL
JANUARY					
FEBRUARY					
MARCH					
APRIL					
MAY					
JUNE					
JULY					
AUGUST					
SEPTEMBER					
OCTOBER					
NOVEMBER					
DECEMBER					

What's Next?

- Reflect on what you've learned in this toolkit. Identify one chapter or topic that resonated most with you and start implementing those strategies today.
- Stay curious! Continue reading, researching, and learning about personal finance. Growth is an ongoing process.
- Share your knowledge. Teaching others what you've learned reinforces your own understanding and creates a ripple effect of financial empowerment.

"Your financial journey is uniquely yours—embrace it with confidence, curiosity, and courage. The future is yours to create."

– Dr Kendall M. Bundy

Made in United States
Orlando, FL
06 November 2026

90241461R00071